Instructor's Manual

Building
Real Life

English Skills

Third Edition

Carolyn Morton Starkey
Norgina Wright Penn

National Textbook Company
a division of *NTC Publishing Group* • Lincolnwood, Illinois USA

Contents

Introduction

Now in a third edition, *Building Real Life English Skills* is designed to help students function effectively in today's increasingly complex world. The text takes English skills, often studied in isolation, and makes them relevant to students' lives by applying them to real world situations.

Many people have difficulty dealing with the printed matter, technological advances, and oral communications required to cope with everyday situations. Government studies have revealed that millions of adults in the United States are functionally illiterate. In addition, many people are unable to do such things as address an envelope correctly. When faced with such tasks as matching personal qualifications with the job requirements presented in classified ads, they often feel overwhelmed.

Building Real Life English Skills helps these people by using actual materials to integrate life skills with traditional classroom skills. The book includes advertisements, contracts, warranties, and agreements that often confront consumers. There are recipes, labels, and product use instructions that are found in virtually any home. In addition, the forms, applications, and techniques that are needed for successful job seeking are included. Presented in a step-by-step sequence, *Building Real Life English Skills* helps students develop confidence as they develop their skills both inside and outside the classroom setting.

Organization of the Book

There are twelve chapters in the text, including Chapter 12, Writer's Workshop. Each of the chapters includes:

- *Words to Know.* Vocabulary introduced in the chapter—terms that may be unfamiliar to the students—supplied with definitions.

- *Practice Activities.* Exercises designed to give students ample practice in the skills and strategies covered.

- *Check Your Understanding.* Review questions that assess students' comprehension of chapter material.

- *Show What You Know.* Hands-on activities that encourage students to apply new knowledge and use higher-order thinking, including creative and critical thinking skills.

Scope of Skills Taught

	Reading Labels	Following Directions	Reading Newspapers	Reading Critically	Understanding Agreements and Warranties	Writing Letters & Consumer Complaints	Getting A Job	Filling Out Forms	Reference Skills	Using Directories	Special Reading Skills	Writing Workshop
READING SKILLS												
• Main Ideas		•	•	•	•						•	•
• Details	•	•	•	•	•	•	•	•	•	•	•	•
• Sequence	•	•				•		•			•	•
• Inferences	•	•	•	•	•			•				
• Drawing Conclusions	•	•		•	•	•				•		
• Comparisons	•				•							
• Classifying Information			•	•					•	•	•	
• Fact and Opinion			•	•								
HIGHER ORDER THINKING SKILLS	•	•	•	•	•	•	•	•	•	•	•	•
VOCABULARY	•	•	•	•	•	•	•	•	•	•	•	•
WRITING SKILLS												
• Abbreviations		•	•			•	•	•				•
• Business Letters						•						
• Personal Letters						•						
• Completing Forms and Applications		•					•	•				
• Writing Messages							•					
• Topic Sentences												•
• Supporting Sentences												•
• Closing Sentences												•
• Paragraphs												•
• Sentence Patterns												•
• Run-on Sentences												•
• Sentence Fragments												•
• Verbs												•
• Tense Shifts												•
• Subject-Verb Agreement												•
• Punctuation												•
• Capitalization												•
• Proofreading												•
REFERENCE SKILLS									•	•		
• Maps										•		
• Schedules										•		
• Charts and Graphs									•	•		
• Tables of Contents			•						•			
• Indexes			•						•		•	
• Dictionary Skills									•			
• Library Skills									•			
• Signs and Directories										•	•	
ORAL COMMUNICATION						•	•					

CHAPTER 1
Reading Labels (p. 1)

Objectives

After completing this chapter the student will be able to:

1. Identify important information on medicine labels.

2. Identify important warnings and precautions on household product labels.

3. Identify important information on clothing labels.

4. Locate specific information on packaged food labels (e.g., net weight, ingredients, calories).

5. Use the information found on labels to answer specific questions about products.

6. Define and use vocabulary words related to labels.

Suggested Activities

1. Consumers now have an option at the marketplace: they can select brand-name labels or the so-called "no name" (generic) label. Even drug items can be bought by their generic names with a savings to the consumer. Have students bring in both brand-name and generic labels for the same product (e.g., DelMonte Corn label and the black-and-white no-name corn label). Have student compare (1) nutrition information, (2) ingredients, and (3) price. Also have students discuss the savings that come with buying generic drugs (prescription medicines). Ask students which consumer groups would benefit most from buying generic drugs. (The elderly often have very high drug costs.) A group of students can research prices by visiting local drug stores and talking with the pharmacists.

2. Over the past few years, "signature" items have been popular with the American buying public. Guess and Major Damaged are only two of the names popular with teens. Discuss "signatures" and other brand names in class. Find out how much students are willing to pay for a label (and why).

3. Pharmacists now attach additional warnings and instructions to the prescription medicines they fill. A local pharmacist will probably provide you with a set of these adhesive labels for classroom use. Some of the most common ones follow. Have students discuss the purpose of these labels.

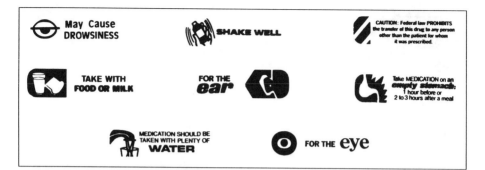

4. Have students write the FTC in Washington, DC, for more information on labels. Refer to Chapter 6, Writing Letters and Consumer Complaints, for letter-writing style. The class can be divided into groups according to the type of label (medicine, clothing, household product, food) for which they are requesting information. A student from each group can give an oral report on the group's findings, and a class bulletin board can be used to display all information. Some students may be interestedin finding out more about the Universal Price Code (UPC). These students should write the Food and Drug Administration's Office of Public Affairs, 5600 Fishers Lane, Rockville, MD 20857.

ANSWERS

ACTIVITY 1—Interpreting Labels on Over-the-Counter Medicines (p. 3)

Bufferin Label

1. Bufferin - Arthritis Strength

2. minor aches and pains, stiffness, swelling and inflammation of arthritis

3. two caplets

4. every six hours; eight caplets

5. if pain or fever persists or gets worse; if new symptoms occur, or if redness or swelling is present

6. see red underlined on label

Vicks DayCare Label

1. Vicks DayCare (cold medicine)

2. stuffy nose, congested sinus openings, headache pain, cough, irritated throat

3. adults: one fluid ounce (2 tablespoonfuls); children: one-half fluid ounce (1 tablespoonful)

4. every four hours; four doses per day (or 8 tablespoonfuls)

5. persistent cough, high fever

6. (a) do not use without consulting a physician if you have high blood pressure, diabetes, heart or thyroid disease; (b) do not use more than 10 days unless directed by physician; (c) do not exceed recommended dosage unless directed by physician

ACTIVITY 2—Interpreting Labels on Prescription Medicines (p. 5)

Sam's Drugs Label No. 2345

1. Geri Purshing

2. Two

3. Dr. Pillston

4. four

5. 0 (no)

Sam's Drugs Label No. 2346

1. Vicki Urkan

2. One

3. Dr. Jaons

4. six

5. 0 (no)

Check Your Understanding of Medicine Labels (p. 6)

1. side effect

2. symptom

3. caution

4. dose

5. physician, prescription

SHOW WHAT YOU KNOW... About Medicine Labels (p. 7)

Answers will vary.

ACTIVITY 3—Reading Labels on Household Products (p. 8)

Roxo Bleach Label

1. F

2. F

3. T

4. T

5. F

Flying Insect Killer Label

1. F

2. F

3. T

4. F

5. F

6. F

7. T

8. T

9. F

10. T

ACTIVITY 4—Reading Labels on Household Products (p. 10)

Ammonia Label

1. Rinse eyes thoroughly with water, preferably warm, for 15 minutes.

2. Give large quantities of diluted vinegar or juice of lemon, grapefruit, or orange. Call physician.

3. Flood with water, then wash with vinegar.

4. Flood with water, then wash with vinegar.

Red Demon Lye Label

1. Immediately hold face under running water for 20 minutes with eyes open, by force if necessary.

2. Clear mouth. Do not induce vomiting. Give (drink) large quantities of water or milk. Give at least 2 ounces to maximum of one pint equal parts of vinegar and water, followed by olive oil or cooking oil (by teaspoon). Transport victim to nearest medical facility or call physician immediately.

3. Flush with water for 15 minutes.

4. Flush with water for 15 minutes.

Check Your Understanding of Household Products Labels (p. 11)

1. Spray surface generously. Wipe immediately with a clean dry cloth.

2. container may burst

3. shake well

4. near fire or flame

5. container may burst

6. about six inches

7. no

SHOW WHAT YOU KNOW...
About Labels on Household Products (p. 12)

Answers will vary.

ACTIVITY 5—Reading Clothing Labels (p.13)

1. F

2. T

3. F

4. T

5. T

ACTIVITY 6—Reading Clothing Labels (p. 14)

1. B

2. A, D, H

3. C, D, H

4. A

5. A, D, E, G, H (note: label G is only label specifying "line-dry only")

6. F, G

7. A, E, G,

8. F

Check Your Understanding of Clothing Labels (p. 15)

1. material treated to hold its shape and resist wrinkling (material that is 60% polyester and 40% cotton)

2. wash with items similar in color

3. no

4. yes

5. no

SHOW WHAT YOU KNOW... About Clothing Labels (p. 15)

Answers will vary.

ACTIVITY 7—Reading Food Labels (p. 18)

Cost Cutter Corn Label

1. one cup

2. two

3. 210

4. A; C

5. 6(%)

6. calcium

Kroger Mixed Vegetables

1. one cup

2. approximately one

3. 70

4. 2;14

5. fat

6. A; C

7. 4(%)

8. carrots, potatoes, celery, sweet peas, green beans, corn, lima beans, water, salt, ground onion

9. 8$\frac{1}{2}$ oz.

10. 8(%)

ACTIVITY 8—Reading and Comparing Food Labels (p. 20)

1. 8

2. 80

3. 19g (grams)

4. aspartame (NutraSweet)

5. no

6. Sugar Free Jell-O: gelatin, adipic acid, maltodextrin, disodium phosphate, aspartame, fumaric acid, artificial color, salt, artificial flavor

   Regular Jell-O: sugar, gelatin, adipic acid, disodium phosphate, fumaric acid, artificial color, artificial flavor

7. General Foods Corporation, White Plains, NY 10625

Check Your Understanding of Food Labels (p. 22)

1. 40

2. tomatoes

3. two

4. 2(%)

5. A

SHOW WHAT YOU KNOW... About Food Labels (p. 23)

Answers will vary.

CHAPTER 2
Following Directions (p. 24)

Objectives

After completing this chapter the student will be able to:

1. Read and follow general directions.

2. Read and follow sequential directions and instructions.

3. Read and follow recipe directions.

4. Read and follow test directions.

5. Use the "grid" method correctly on test booklets and answer sheets.

6. Explain and use the process of elimination in attempting to answer multiple choice questions on tests.

7. Identify and use specific words and phrases (e.g., always, never, best) when answering multiple choice questions.

8. Define and use words related to directions and instructions, recipes, and test-taking.

Suggested Activities

1. This chapter does not cover oral directions. Have students choose partners. One student is to request directions from his or her partner for walking from one given point to another. Prepare index cards in advance and make a game out of this activity. Divide the class into teams. Each team scores points based on how well it gives directions. A neutral panel of students can score the teams. Emphasis should be on lefts, rights, number of blocks, traffic lights, landmarks, etc. The students can also discuss how their directions would differ if the person requesting directions were driving.

2. Try to secure sample SAT, ACT, or GRE tests for your students to practice following test directions. The publishers handling these tests may provide samples upon request. Also, libraries carry a number of books to help students prepare for the tests. These books often carry sample tests. Be sure students planning to take

the ACT, SAT, or a state competency test get practice in sentence completions, antonyms, analogies, and reading passages.

3. Use this chapter to improve your students' verbal communication skills. Have one or two students demonstrate how to make or do something in front of the class. Then have another student follow these directions. Some suggestions are: writing in calligraphy, using a microscope, potting a plant, or performing a card trick.

4. Have students make up recipe cards and write their own recipes. Be sure each recipe card lists ingredients and gives complete directions.

ANSWERS

ACTIVITY 1—Reading Directions (p. 25)

1. a

2. c

3. a

4. c

5. b

ACTIVITY 2—Following Step-by-Step Directions (p. 26)

See folded letter in Step 1 (p. 26)
See folded letter in Step 2 (p. 27)

ACTIVITY 3—Following Directions (p. 27)

1. F		**6.** T	
2. F		**7.** T	
3. T		**8.** T	
4. F		**9.** F	
5. T		**10.** T	

ACTIVITY 4—Sequential Directions—Setting a Digital Watch (p. 29)

Setting the Month

1 Press the SET button once.

4 Release the TIME button when the number of the desired month appears.

3 Hold the TIME button down.

2 Look for a flashing month number indicating you are in the "month set mode."

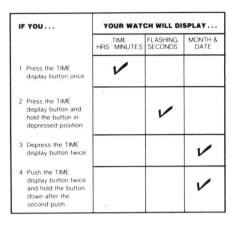

IF YOU...	YOUR WATCH WILL DISPLAY...		
	TIME HRS MINUTES	FLASHING SECONDS	MONTH & DATE
1 Press the TIME display button once	✔		
2 Press the TIME display button and hold the button in depressed position		✔	
3 Depress the TIME display button twice			✔
4 Push the TIME display button twice and hold the button down after the second push			✔

Setting the Date

1 Press the SET button a second time.

4 Release the TIME button when the correct date appears.

3 Hold the TIME button down.

2 Look for a flashing date indicating you are in the "date set mode."

Setting Hours

1 Press the SET button a third time.

4 Release the TIME button when the correct hour is displayed.

3 Hold the TIME button down.

2 Look for a flashing date indicating you are in the "hours set mode."

Setting Minutes

1 Press the SET button a fourth time.

4 Release the TIME button when the correct minute appears.

3 Hold the TIME button down.

2 Look for a flashing minute indicating you are in the "minute set mode."

SHOW WHAT YOU KNOW... About Following Directions (p. 33)

For this activity, the teacher should circulate the room and evaluate each group separately. Another alternative is to have each group present before the class and evaluate each on clarity and completeness.

ACTIVITY 5—Understanding Recipe Vocabulary (p. 35)

1. c

2. e

3. a

4. d

5. f

6. b

ACTIVITY 6—Understanding Recipe Abbreviations (p. 36)

1. oz.

2. c.

3. gal.

4. lb.

5. tbsp.

6. qt.

7. tsp. or t.

8. dz.

9. sm.

10. pt.

11. pkg.

12. sq.

13. lg.

14. min.

ACTIVITY 7—Reading Recipe Directions (p. 36)

Pound Cake Recipe

1. One-half pound of (butter)

2. Five; one at a time

3. tube

4. one hour and 30 minutes; 350 degrees

5. fifteen

6. cold

Veg-A-Burger Recipe

1. 8-oz. can

2. cup

3. uncooked

4. drained

5. hamburger; onions

6. six

ACTIVITY 8—Reading Recipe Directions (p. 38)

Lemon Sponge Pie

1. no

2. yes

3. no

4. no

5. no

6. yes

Pizza

1. no

2. no

3. yes

4. yes

5. no

6. no

Check Your Understanding of Recipes (p. 40)

1. cup

2. teaspoon

3. quart

4. teaspoon

5. small

6. gallon

7. dozen

8. pound

9. tablespoon

10. pint

11. set oven temperature in advance

12. mash or beat until smooth

13. shred with a grater

14. heat to just below the boiling point

15. cook at low heat on top of stove

SHOW WHAT YOU KNOW... About Recipes (p. 40)

Answers will vary.

ACTIVITY 9—Completing Test Booklet Covers (p. 43)

Answers will vary.

ACTIVITY 10—Following Test Directions (p. 45)

1. 4721 _____√_____ 4721

2. 584 _____√_____ 584

3. 80962 _____ 90862

4. 9325 _____√_____ 9325

5. 0365 _____ 0356

6. Louis Eldern _____√_____ Louis Eldern

7. James Meyer _____ James Mayer

8. Arthur Lungren _____ Arthur Lundgren

9. Frank Schaefer ___√___ Frank Schaefer

10. Allan Kenmore _____ Albert Kenmore

ACTIVITY 11—Following Test Directions (p. 46)

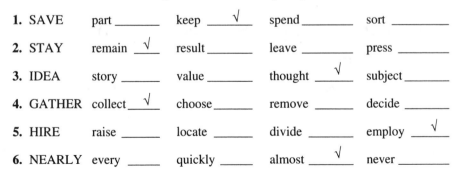

1. SAVE   part _____   keep ___√___   spend _____   sort _____

2. STAY   remain __√__   result _____   leave _____   press _____

3. IDEA   story _____   value _____   thought __√__   subject _____

4. GATHER collect __√__   choose _____   remove _____   decide _____

5. HIRE   raise _____   locate _____   divide _____   employ __√__

6. NEARLY every _____   quickly _____   almost __√__   never _____

ACTIVITY 12—Answering Multiple-Choice Questions (p. 50)

1. A

2. C

3. A

4. A

5. D

Check Your Understanding of Taking Tests (p. 51)

1. applicant

2. tester

3. multiple-choice

4. horizontal

5. SAT

6. vertical

7. T

8. T

9. F

10. T

SHOW WHAT YOU KNOW... About Taking Tests (p. 52)

Inside of Paper	Outside of Paper
Teacher's Name	Student's Name

CHAPTER 3
Reading Newspapers (p. 53)

Objectives

After completing this chapter the student will be able to:

1. Locate information in a newspaper by using its index.

2. Answer specific questions about a news event after reading a news story.

3. Separate the facts from the opinions in an editorial.

4. Distinguish a news story (article) from an editorial.

5. Identify who, what, when, and where in a nrew story.

6. Use the information found in classified ads to answer specific questions about these ads.

7. Explain the meaning of abbreviations used in job ads.

8. Use recall and context clues to figure out the meaning of abbreviations used in apartment and used car ads.

9. Locate job openings in the help wanted section of the newspaper that match the student's own experience.

10. Define and use vocabulary words related to the newspaper.

Suggested Activities

1. Have each student locate a news story and an editorial on the same topic. Read some of these in class. Discuss the differences.

2. Have students write letters to the editor or publisher of their local newspaper(s) on an issue that concerns them, their families, or the local community. Refer to Chapter 6, Writing Letters and Consumer Complaints, for letter-writing style.

3. Have students study the classified ads in their local newspaper and bring to class a list of classified ad words and abbreviations for these categories: Jobs (Employ-

ment), Houses & Apartments for Rent, Merchandise for Sale. Students are to make a list of abbreviations with the abbreviations written out.

4. Most newspapers sell ad space to readers. Within the classified ad section there is often a form provided for readers to write their own ads. Students should practice filling out these forms in class. Emphasize (1) length (using key words), (2) necessary information (what is for sale and how to reach the seller), and (3) cost (the more words, the more an ad costs). Students can create their own classified ad paper and circulate it within class. (This gives the students an opportunity to use their writing skills to make money.)

ANSWERS

ACTIVITY 1—Using the Newspaper Index (p. 54)

Sports	Editorial	Classified Ads	Entertainment	Home Section
4, 5	7	9	1, 3, 6, 8	2, 10

ACTIVITY 2—Using the Newspaper Index (p. 55)

Topics	Pages	Section
How to grow house plants	1, 2	L
Tours to Las Vegas	1-6	J
What's in store for a Gemini today	19	C
Stamp Collecting	5	J
Job openings	1-8 (F) or 1-8(G)	F, G
Your favorite comic strip	2-8(L)	L
Stock averages	3-6	E

ACTIVITY 3—Reading News Stories (p. 56)

Girls Don't Lag in Math

1. girls' ability to do math

2. A study was conducted by researchers from the University of Chicago.

3. to disprove, or contradict, the Johns Hopkins University study

4. Zalman Usiskin and two colleagues tested 1,366 high school students in geometry after both the boys and girls had been taught the material.

5. in classrooms across the country

6. 1,366

7. no

8. Scholastic Aptitude Tests (SAT)

9. Zalman Usiskin, Sharon Senk, and Roberta Dees

10. geometry

Pupils Go to Mat in Academic Olympics

1. a fourth-grader at Dodge Elementary School, 2651 W. Washington Blvd.

2. became a champion in the District 9 Academic Olympics

3. West Side District (Crane High School auditorium, 2245 W. Jackson Blvd.)

4. They wanted to "elevate the achievement levels of their pupils."

5. the inner-city school districts

ACTIVITY 4—Editorials and News Stories: "Facts vs. Opinion" (p. 59)

1. Editorial

2. News Story

3. Editorial

4. News Story

5. Editorial

6. News Story

7. Editorial

8. News Story

9. News Story

10. Editorial

ACTIVITY 5—Reading Editorials (p. 60)

1. disturbances by youngsters riding motorcycles

2. A child's parents should be held responsible for a child's actions while riding a motorcycle.

3. The sheriff has decided not to respond to calls complaining about youngsters riding motorcycles.

4. Answers will vary.

ACTIVITY 6—Reading the "Classifieds" (p. 61)

Apartment Ads

1. $435

2. yes

3. 374-2836

4. studio, 1 bedroom, 2 bedrooms, 2 bedrooms with den and 2 baths

5. the studio

6. 2 bedrooms with den and 2 baths

7.

rm.	room
H/HW	heat/hot water
sec.	security
mod.	modern
avail.	available
immed. occup	immediate occupancy
pref.	preferred
cpl.	couple

Car Ads

1.

ps	power steering
pb	power brakes
lo. mi.	low mileage
gar. kept	garage kept
exc. cond.	excellent condition
a/c	air conditioner
r/def.	rear defroster

2. one

3. $1500

4. $14,300

5. three

6. 4-door, V6 engine, air conditioning, power steering, power brakes, am/fm radio, tilt wheel, cruise control

7. car dealership (WOODFIELD LEXUS)

8. It has a lot of options (extras).

9. The seller does not want to settle for less than the asking price.

Check Your Understanding of Reading Newspapers (p. 63)

1. index

2. classified ad

3. editorial

4. alphabetical

5. obituary

6. feature

7. F

8. F (some urban newspapers might carry restaurant ads by neighborhood in their classified section)

9. T

10. T

SHOW WHAT YOU KNOW... About Reading Newspapers (p. 63)

Answers will vary.

ACTIVITY 7—Reading Want Ad Abbreviations (p. 65)

1. g

2. f

3. a

4. c

5. j

6. b

7. d

8. i

9. h

10. e

ACTIVITY 8—Reading Want Ad Abbreviations (p. 65)

1. Apartment Manager
Experienced for new high-rise building. Salary, apartment, and incentives.

2. Secretary
For appliance store. Answer phone, file, no experience necessary, but must type 60 words per minute.

3. Fitters
5 years experience. Good wages and benefits.

4. Die Makers
Day work. Full benefits.

5. Quality Control Assistant
Two years experience required in automotive. Good wages, benefits.

6. Lab Technician
All-around plate man. Permanent position, excellent conditions and salary.

SHOW WHAT YOU KNOW… About Help-Wanted Ads (p. 67)

Answers will vary.

ACTIVITY 9—Reading Want Ads for Information (p. 68)

1. dishwasher, pizza maker

2. 222 Lane St.; 2:30–5:30 P.M.

3. Acme Personnel

4. 555-9683

5. hard shoes

ACTIVITY 10—Looking for Specific Jobs in the Want Ads (p. 68)

Ads and answers will vary.

ACTIVITY 11—Using the Help-Wanted Section of the Newspaper (p. 69)

1. 555-7870

2. one

3. Box C-1605, Local Press, Springfield

4. 555-6801

5. Stock Person (Arcade Attendant and Cashier ads also acceptable)

6. Job Finders, Inc.

Check Your Understanding of Help-Wanted Ads (p. 70)

1. experienced	**6.** education	**11.** c
2. assistant	**7.** part-time	**12.** c
3. preferred	**8.** weekly	**13.** c
4. salary	**9.** trainee	**14.** a
5. secretary	**10.** department	**15.** b

CHAPTER 4
Reading Critically (p. 71)

Objectives

After completing this chapter the student will be able to:

1. Identify the techniques used in various advertisements.

2. Answer questions about information found in product advertisements.

3. Separate facts from opinions in advertisements.

4. Identify both specific information and generalities in advertisements.

5. Name and give an example of at least three advertising techniques.

6. Select important details from special offers.

7. Describe the obligations of the buyer in membership offers.

8. Locate specific information in magazine subscription offers.

9. Locate the expiration date on coupon offers.

10. Define and use vocabulary words related to advertisements and special offers.

Suggested Activities

1. Conduct a coupon exchange. Have students bring to class coupons they find in newspapers and magazines. Put all the savings coupons in a coupon exchange basket. Place the basket in a central location. Students can take coupons from the basket for savings. All students should contribute to the exchange. As students select and exchange coupons, they learn about the limits and conditions that come with coupon savings.

2. Ask each student to bring in a sample of a good advertisement and a sample of an ad he or she rates as very poor. The poorly rated ads may contain lies and half-truths, use too many advertising techniques, or lack the information necessary to make a wise buying decision. Discuss in detail the advertisements that represent inferior advertising practices.

3. Have students keep a record of TV commercials for two consecutive days. Use the contents of these commercials to help students develop critical listening skills. Use the following discussion questions to help students evaluate commercials and explore (and evaluate) their own buying habits:

- How long is the average commercial?

- Which commercials appealed to you? Why?

- Which commercials did not appeal to you? Why not?

- Did the products seem to have any connection to the type of audience that would most likely be watching the sponsored program?

- Did any of the commercials that were endorsements by famous people appeal to you? If so, which ones? Why?

- Did you find any commercials demeaning to a specific group of people (women, men, African Americans, Hispanics, senior citizens)? Explain.

- Why do you think a particular celebrity is chosen to endorse a particular product?

4. Have each student bring in a special offer for a magazine subscription, music (recording/CD/tape) club, videotape club, or book club. Each student is to answer specific questions about the offer:

- How long does the subscription or membership run?

- How much do you pay? When do you begin payment?

- How much do you save?

- What is your obligation, if any?

- Does the ad specify that anyone under eighteen must have the signature of a parent?

- What is your evaluation of this offer?

ANSWERS

ACTIVITY 1—Reading Ads Carefully (p. 73)

Lose Fat Forever Ad

1. Answers will vary.

2. Answers will vary.

Career Certificate Ad

1. no

2. a box number

3. typing, auto mechanics, truck driving, hair styling, catering, barbering, computer programming, driver instructor training

4. Answers will vary.

5. a high school dropout; a high school graduate with no vocational skills; an adult who never attended high school

6. • When you finish the course, your "Career Certificate" will help you get a job.

   • Many people who take a career course earn $50,000 a year.

   • You don't have to worry about money now. The important thing is to enroll for the current semester. You can always pay later.

   • The training is like college. (There are semesters, registration, tuition fees.)

ACTIVITY 2—Reading Ads with Emotional Appeal (p. 76)

1. Intelligent Shoppers Ad: b

2. Hair Color Magic Ad: c

ACTIVITY 3—Reading Ads with Emotional Appeal— "The Famous Person" (p. 76)

1. Answers will vary

2. • I know about *all cars* . . . your car, your brother's car, your mother's car, your Aunt Isabelle's car, my car.

- . . . and I'm tellin' you what your car needs is PST.

- Put PST in your car and you'll run like a champion!

- Use PST in your car and it'll be ready for the Indiana 600 . . .

3. b (a is also acceptable)

ACTIVITY 4—Reading Ads with Emotional Appeal—"Get on the Bandwagon" (p. 78)

1. • Everyone, but Everyone, is chewing Minty-Fresh Gum!

- Join the crowd!

- Try it!

2. The drawing shows a variety of people.

3. Answers will vary. Students should mention making up one's mind is desirable.

ACTIVITY 5—Reading Ads—Specific Information or Glowing Generality? (p. 79)

1. Specific information

2. Glowing generality

3. Glowing generality

4. Specific information

5. Specific information

6. Glowing generality

ACTIVITY 6—Evaluating Popular Advertisements: Finding Out What Types of Ads Appeal to You (p. 80)
Sweet Dreams Ad

1. Answers will vary.

2. Answers will vary.

3. (a) "What would it be like to make the cheerleading squad . . . or win the Olympics . . . or become the most popular girl *ever*?"

(b) if you ever dream about . . . winning beauty contests; Sweet Dreams make my dreams come true.

(c) Every one of them lets me see my dreams come true; If you ever dream about boys, winning beauty contests and becoming famous . . .; You've *got* to read them so you, too, can see *your* dreams come true!

Lustra-Curl Ad

1. vanity—need to look good
(also bandwagon appeal—need to follow the crowd)

2. perfect curls; finest in after-care products

3. Lustrasilk makes at least twelve after-care products (as pictured); Lustrasilk recommends that you ask you hair stylist about the after-care products shown.

4. The Lustra-Curl is the "real curl"; Lustra-Curl gives you versatility for lots of styles; You'll have all the fun . . .

Buf-Oxal Ad

Facts

- Buf-Oxal is a benzoyl peroxide gel.

- Buf-Oxal is available in 5% and 10% strengths.

- Buf-Oxal is water-based.

Opinions

- Zits are the pits.

- Buf-Oxal is gentle.

- You will be surprised at how quickly Buf-Oxal will clean up your pimples,blackheads, and blemishes.

Check Your Understanding of Advertisements (p. 84)

1. guarantee

2. glowing generality

3. vanity

4. bandwagon appeal

5. optional

6. endorse

7. emotional appeal

8. glowing generality

9. not truthful and half-truths

10. sense appeal

SHOW WHAT YOU KNOW... About Advertisements (p. 85)

Answers will vary.

ACTIVITY 7—Interpreting Magazine Subscription Offers (p. 87)

1. T

2. T

3. T

4. T

5. F

ACTIVITY 8—Reading a CD Offer for Details (p. 88)

1. $1.86

2. every four weeks; up to six times per year

3. nothing

4. indicate your preference on the card and mail it back by the date specified

5. 10 days

6. yes

7. yes

8. the club

9. $12.98-$15.98; $6.95

10. after you have completed your membership agreement (to buy 6 more selections anytime during the next three years)

ACTIVITY 9—Reading a Book Club Offer for Details (p. 90)

1. four

2. $2 plus shipping and handling costs

3. 10

4. yes; there is a shipping and handling cost

5. 15 times a year (about every $3^1/_2$ weeks)

6. four

7. mark the reply form and return it by the specified date

ACTIVITY 10—Reading Coupon Offers (p. 91)

1. Cheerios cereal; Bold Hold hair spray

2. Cheerios: yes, 10 oz. or larger; Bold Hold: no

3. no

4. Bold Hold: yes, 2/28/93; Cheerios: yes 3/15/88

ACTIVITY 11—Reading Refund and Free Coupon Offers (p. 92)

Burger King Coupon

1. $1.00

2. no

3. no

4. 11

Mail-In Certificate

1. $2.00 cash refund

2. yes; UPC symbols from any 3 Betty Crocker products listed on the coupon and the coupon itself

3. $2.00 in cash

4. General Mills, Inc., Box 5237, Minneapolis, MN 55460

5. up to 6 weeks

6. May 31, 1988

Check Your Understanding of Special Offers (p. 93)

1. coupon

2. expiration date

3. obligation

4. refund

5. discount

6. redeem

7. T

8. T

9. T

10. F

SHOW WHAT YOU KNOW... About Special Offers (p. 94)

Answers will vary.

CHAPTER 5

Understanding Agreements and Warranties (p. 95)

Objectives

After completing this chapter the student will be able to:

1. Select important details in agreements, contracts, and warranties.

2. Interpret the language of credit agreements.

3. Match various terms and conditions with specific contracts or agreements.

4. State whether a given warranty is limited or full.

5. List what is covered and what is not covered in a new car warranty.

6. Define and use vocabulary words related to agreements and contracts and warranties.

Suggested Activities

1. Legal documents mentioned in this chapter but not discussed include wills, deeds, and birth certificates. Secure samples of these and other documents for class discussion. Some other documents that might interest the class are marriage licenses, court summonses, apartment leases, car titles, and employment agency contracts.

2. Make up a word search puzzle using either warranty words or agreement and contract words. Distribute copies to the class.

ANSWERS

ACTIVITY 1—Using Credit Terms (p. 97)

1. installment

2. interest

3. percentage rate

4. disclosure

5. creditor

6. down payment

7. co-maker

8. default

9. delinquent

10. debts

ACTIVITY 2—Reading Credit Agreements (p. 97)

1. c

2. c (a is also acceptable)

3. c

4. c

ACTIVITY 3—Using Agreements and Contract Words (p. 98)

A. 3

B. 2

C. 7

D. 8

E. 9

F. 1

G. 10

H. 6

I. 5

J. 4

ACTIVITY 4—Reading Terms on Charge Accounts (p. 99)

1. F

2. T

3. T

4. F

5. T

6. T

7. T

8. T

9. T

10. F

ACTIVITY 5—Reading Agreements (p. 102)

1. c

2. f

3. f

4. a

5. c

6. d

7. e

8. e

9. b

10. a

Check Your Understanding of Agreements and Contracts (p. 103)

1. c

2. a

3. a

4. a

5. b

6. b

7. b

8. b

9. a

10. c

SHOW WHAT YOU KNOW... About Agreements and Contracts (p. 104)

Answers will vary.

ACTIVITY 6—Using Warranty Words (p. 106)

1. H

2. E

3. F

4. A

5. C

6. B

7. G

8. D

ACTIVITY 7—Using Warranty Words (p. 106)

1. manufacturer

2. full warranty

3. limited warranty

4. prepaid

5. defects; authorized dealer

ACTIVITY 8—Reading Warranties for Details (p. 107)

1. Sharp CB

2. Sharp Electronics Corp., 10 Keystone Place, Paramus, NJ 07651

3. defects in workmanship and materials

4. one year

5. return it to the manufacturer at address on warranty

ACTIVITY 9—Reading Warranties for Details (p. 108)

1. F

2. T

3. F

4. T

5. F

6. F

7. T

8. F

9. T

10. T

ACTIVITY 10—Reading a Car Warranty (p. 109)

What Is Covered

1. c

2. d

3. d

4. c

What Is Not Covered

1. Any combination of three of the following is acceptable: collision, fire, theft, freezing, vandalism, riot, explosion, objects striking the car, driving over curbs, overloading, racing or other competition, alterations to the car

2. Any combination of two of the following is acceptable: airborne fallout (chemicals, tree sap, etc.), stones, hail, earthquake, water or flood, windstorm, lightning

3. the owner (buyer)

4. The Maintenance Schedule and Owner's Manual explain when maintenance is needed.

Check Your Understanding of Warranties (p. 111)

1. c

2. a

3. b

4. c

5. c

6. a

7. a

8. b

9. b

10. b

SHOW WHAT YOU KNOW... About Warranties (p. 112)

Answers will vary.

CHAPTER 6
Writing Letters and Consumer Complaints (p. 113)

Objectives

After completing this chapter the student will be able to:

1. Write a personal or business letter using the correct format.

2. Address an envelope to include a complete return address and destination address.

3. Correctly use state abbreviations.

4. Describe the specific information needed to handle a complaint by telephone (e.g., name, address, telephone number, names of persons involved).

5. Write a letter of complaint using the correct format and including all the information necessary to resolve the complaint.

6. Name at least five places a person can take a consumer complaint.

7. Define and use vocabulary words related to writing letters and consumer complaints.

Suggested Activities

1. The U.S. Postal Service in cooperation with the National Council of Teachers of English (NCTE) has published a booklet that contains information about letter writing. *All About Letters* contains information on consumer complaint letters, celebrity letters, ZIP Codes, pen pal organizations, address abbreviations, and many other topics related to letter writing. It would be a useful classroom supplement to this chapter. The booklet may be available at your local or school library, or you can write or call the U.S. Postal Service or the NCTE, 1111 Kenyon Road, Urbana, IL 61801, for more information on how to secure this booklet.

2. *The Consumer Information Catalog* lists a number of free government publications. Each student can write to the Consumer Information Center, Pueblo, CO 81009, for a copy of this catalog. When the catalogs arrive, have students order the booklets that interest them.

ANSWERS

ACTIVITY 1—Personal Letters of Thanks (p. 115)

Letters will vary. They should include a heading, salutation, specific message, appropriate closing, and signature.

ACTIVITY 2—Writing a Personal Letter (p. 115)

Letters will vary. They should include a heading, salutation, body, appropriate closing, and signature.

ACTIVITY 3—Writing a Letter of Invitation (p. 115)

Letters will vary. They should include a heading; salutation; body that includes who, what, when, where, and why; closing; and signature.

ACTIVITY 4—Writing a Business Letter (p. 117)

Letters will vary. They should include a heading, inside address, salutation, closing, and signature.

For letter **a**, students should include the name of the product and clearly state why they use (or no longer use) it.

For letter **b**, students should include when they are available and when and how they can be contacted. Some students may include what they think they can do for the organization.

For letter **c**, students should make clear that they wish to cancel their memberships. Some students may spell out why they wish to cancel (e.g., have completed membership obligations, are dissatisfied with the product or offer).

ACTIVITY 5—Addressing Envelopes (p. 120)

The second envelope is correct. It includes the state and ZIP Code in the destination.

ACTIVITY 6—Addressing Envelopes (p. 121)

See page 41.

ACTIVITY 7—Using State Abbreviations (p. 121)

(Answers are in alphabetical order by state name.)
AL; AK; AZ; CA; CO; CT; DE; DC; FL; GA; HI; ID; IL; IN; IA; KS; KY; LA; ME;
MD; MA; MI; MN; MS; MO; MT; NE; NV; NH; NJ; NM; NY; NC; ND; OH; OK;
OR; PA; RI; SC; SD; TN; TX; UT; VT; VA; WA; WV; WI; WY

Check Your Understanding of Writing Letters (p. 123)

Letters will vary. They should include a heading, inside address, appropriate salutation, body that requests a copy of the *U.S. Government Books Catalog,* closing, and
signature.

SHOW WHAT YOU KNOW… About Writing Letters (p. 122)

Letters will vary.

ACTIVITY 8—Defining Consumer Complaint Words (p. 124)

1. H

2. G

3. A

4. B

5. C

6. D

7. E

8. F

9. J

10. I

ACTIVITY 9—Using Consumer Complaint Words (p. 125)

1. complaint

2. franchise

Stanley Smith
2375 Cherry Lane
Squire, WV 24884

Miss Patricia Lee
417 West Street
Lamont, OK   70215

Michael Dudley
3245 Euclid Avenue
Detroit, MI 48206

Mr. Michael Harper
201 Northland Drive
Yonkers, NY 10101

(Students should use state abbreviations on envelopes.)

3. retailer

4. Food and Drug Administration

5. Better Business Bureau

6. consumer

ACTIVITY 10—Handling Your Complaints (p. 127)

1. E

2. B

3. C

4. H

5. G

6. F

7. A

8. D

ACTIVITY 11—Deciding Where to Go with a Complaint (p. 128)

1. the merchant who sold you the product

2. your state consumer protection agency, State Attorney General's Office, or the Office of Consumer Affairs

3. in the capital city of the state

4. Washington, DC

5. Small Claims Court

6. the Better Business Bureau

ACTIVITY 12—What Action Would *You* Take? (p. 128)

Answers will vary but may include some of these approaches:

1. Action might include: contact the manager of the authorized dealer; contact the manufacturer; contact the Better Business Bureau; try another authorized dealer. If students interpret the situation to mean that they have already paid for the repairs, they might go to the Small Claims Court to recover the cost of the repairs.

2. Action might include: contact the Better Business Bureau; contact the state or local consumer protection agency; contact the State Attorney General's Office.

3. Action might include: contact the manager of the delivery company; contact the store that sold the furniture; contact the Better Business Bureau; contact the state or local consumer protection agency; contact the State Attorney General's Office. If students interpret the situation to mean that the furniture was simply being moved from one location to another, they might check the moving contract to determine who is responsible for paying for damages and to what amount. If students interpret the situation to mean that they have already paid for repairs or replacement, they might go to the Small Claims Court to recover the cost.

4. Action might include: check the dry cleaning receipt to see if the terms and conditions limit the cleaner's responsibility for buttons; contact the Better Business Bureau; contact the cleaners' business association.

5. Action might include: contact the manager of the radio station to lodge a complaint; write a letter to the editor of the local newspaper(s); contact concerned neighborhood organizations; contact the Federal Communications Commission (FCC).

ACTIVITY 13—Handling a Complaint by Phone (p. 130)

First Version

1. Students will probably rate this call poorly and find that it is ineffective. Joe's angry and accusatory tone simply annoys Kathy and does not remedy the situation.

2. Joe annoyed Kathy and did not resolve the issue of the cold and late pizza.

3. Answers will vary. Students might indicate that they would have tried a different tone or would have demanded a replacement pizza.

Second Version

1. Students will probably rate this call higher than the first version and find that it was effective.

2. Joe took his complaint to the proper person, did not lose his temper, and got a replacement pizza.

3. Answers will vary. Students may or may not think they would have handled the call the way Joe did.

ACTIVITY 14—Writing a Letter of Complaint (p. 132)

Letters will vary. They should include a heading, inside address, salutation, closing, and signature.

For the first letter, students should include a description of the damaged sugar bowl and their account number (8611-003-32-4) and indicate that they want a replacement.

For the second letter, students should include a description of the pair of shoes and the problem, explain the action already taken, and indicate that they want a refund.

Check Your Understanding of Complaints (p. 133)

1. c

2. b

3. b

4. a

5. b

SHOW WHAT YOU KNOW... About Complaints (p. 134)

Letters will vary. They should include a heading, inside address, appropriate salutation, body that includes the name of the program and the specific complaint, closing, and signature.

CHAPTER 7
Getting A Job (p. 135)

Objectives

After completing this chapter the student will be able to:

1. Complete a personal fact sheet.

2. Write a detailed and brief resume.

3. Write a letter of application.

4. Complete a variety of job application forms.

5. Identify responses that would be evaluated as favorable or unfavorable by an interviewer.

6. Identify at least five ways of preparing for a job interview.

7. Ask appropriate questions in a phone job inquiry, based on the information provided in the ad.

8. Write office memos that are brief and complete.

9. Define and use vocabulary words related to the job search.

Suggested Activities

1. It is easy to *discuss* what should be done in a job interview, but doing (and saying) the right thing takes skill and practice. Following is a profile of Bobby Taylor, a sixteen-year-old high-school student looking for part-time work. Read this profile to the class and have them discuss how Bobby handled specific interview questions from the manager at Burger Barn.

PROFILE

Robert E. Taylor
Student: King City High School
Course of Study: Cooperative Education—Business
Age: 16

Bobby Taylor wants to begin saving money for college. He is in his junior year at King High. Burger Barn has part-time openings. It is also close to Bobby's house, so he could walk to work and save gas or bus fare. Bobby plans to study business and finance in college. His dream is to own his own business. The Cooperative Education course at his school has taught him lots of business skills. One of these skills is using the new computerized cash register like the ones at Burger Barn. Bobby's friend and neighbor is Angelica Lopez. Angelica is an assistant manager at Burger Barn. She told Bobby about the opening.

In the interview with the manager at Burger Barn, Bobby was asked several questions. Ask students how they would rate Bobby's responses—favorably or unfavorably. How do they feel the interviewer will respond to Bobby's answers? What would their response have been in Bobby's situation?

1. Manager's Question: "Why do you want to work at Burger Barn?"

   Bobby's Response: "I need the money."

2. Manager's Question: "What hours would you like to work?"

   Bobby's Response: "I'm still in school. My last class is over at 1:00. I guess I'd be able to work any time from 1:00 until you close at 11:00."

3. Manager's Question: "How many hours a day would you be interested in working?"

   Bobby's Response: "As many as I can."

4. Manager's Question: "What about your school work? Will you be able to keep up? Generally, we only like high-school students to work four to five hours per day."

   Bobby's Response: "Four to five hours will be fine."

5. Manager's Question: "We have two openings. One is at the burger grill; the other is cashier. The pay rate is the same for each job. Which do you prefer?"

   Bobby's Response: "Cashier."

6. Manager's Question: "I noticed that you were on time for the interview today. I like that! Many of our student workers are late for work. This can affect our entire schedule. Will transportation be a problem for you? Did you have any difficulty getting here today?"

Bobby's Response: "As a matter of fact, I live just six blocks from here. I can either walk to work or take the local bus."

2. Students may need additional practice in using telephone communications skills. The following job can be used to help sharpen those telephone interview skills they will need in the job search. Read the ads aloud, and then have students role play the interview process. One student plays the caller, and a partner plays the person receiving the call. The class can discuss and evaluate these telephone interviews.

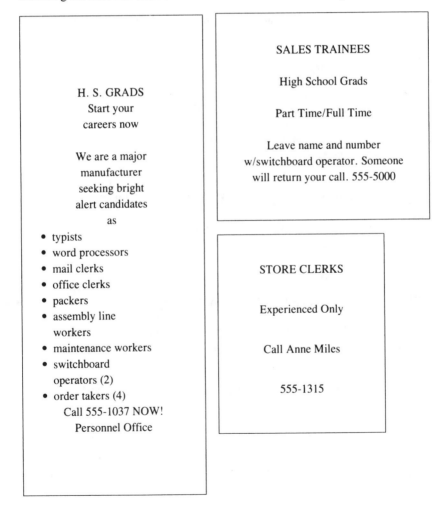

H. S. GRADS
Start your
careers now

We are a major
manufacturer
seeking bright
alert candidates
as

- typists
- word processors
- mail clerks
- office clerks
- packers
- assembly line
  workers
- maintenance workers
- switchboard
  operators (2)
- order takers (4)
  Call 555-1037 NOW!
  Personnel Office

SALES TRAINEES

High School Grads

Part Time/Full Time

Leave name and number
w/switchboard operator. Someone
will return your call. 555-5000

STORE CLERKS

Experienced Only

Call Anne Miles

555-1315

3. Have two students read the following telephone conversation. Other students in the class are to take notes on the conversation and then write the message in the form of a call memo. Refer to the telephone message form in the text for the format.

School Secretary:	"Hello. Central High School."
Parent:	"Hello. I'd like to talk with the principal, please."
School Secretary:	"Dr. Jones is not in the office at this time."
Parent:	"This is Mrs. Barrister, Elaine Barrister. I'd like to speak with her tomorrow about my son, John. Do I need an appointment?"
School Secretary:	"Dr. Jones will be in the office all morning. You can see her between nine and noon."
Parent:	"I'll be in at 10 o'clock."
School Secretary:	"All right, Mrs. Barrister. We'll expect you at 10 o'clock."

ANSWERS

ACTIVITY 1—Making a Personal Fact Sheet (p. 137)

Fact sheets will vary but should include the kinds of information in the sample on p. 136 of the student text.

ACTIVITY 2—Writing a Detailed Job Resume (p. 140)

Resumes will vary but should include personal information (name, address, phone number), educational background, employment history, special skills, special interests, and references.

ACTIVITY 3—Writing a Brief Resume (p. 141)

Resumes will vary but should include personal information, the position applied for, experience, education, and references. They should be no more than one page long.

ACTIVITY 4—Understanding Letters of Application (p. 142)

1. secretarial

2. Personnel Director

3. three years of secretarial training with typing and shorthand speeds of 60 and 120 words per minute; two years work experience as a part-time secretary

4. to talk with Mr. Benawra about a secretarial position in the main office of the Superior Manufacturing Company

5. by writing him at 126 Rockford Street, Chinaville, Ohio 44507, or calling 555-8181

6. a resume

7. part-time secretary for two years

8. yes; Malcolm X High School

9. 60 words per minute

10. 126 Rockford Street, Chinaville, Ohio 44507

SHOW WHAT YOU KNOW... About Letters of Application (p. 144)

Letters will vary. They should be in proper business letter format and include a statement of interest in a specific position, a brief statement of abilities (including a reference to the enclosed resume), and information about how and where the student can be reached.

Check Your Understanding of Letters of Application (p. 144)

Letters will vary. They should be in proper business letter format and include a statement of interest in the specific positions advertised, a brief statement of abilities (including a reference to the enclosed resume), and information about how and where the student can be reached.

ACTIVITY 5—Filling Out Job Applications (p. 145)

1. stock worker

2. L.A. High School

3. vocational

4. no

5. typewriter

6. stock

7. full time

8. no

9. no

10. no; the employer did not check the box preceding weight

ACTIVITY 6—Understanding a Job Application Form (p. 147)

Answers will vary. All information except signature should be printed.

1. today's date

2. name, last name first; social security number

3. address should include ZIP Code

4. If address in number 3 is temporary, permanent address including ZIP Code should be printed here; if address in number 3 is permanent, "Same" should be printed here.

5. phone number

6. job title, when student can start, and pay expected

7. "Yes" or "No" to indicate whether or not they are working; indicate if present employers can be contacted

8. Students should indicate if they have ever worked for the company and print the dates.

9. schools attended, graduation dates, and subjects studied (where appropriate)

10. any special subjects studied

11. any military service, including ranks

12. any clubs that do not indicate race, beliefs, or national origin

13. work experience (starting with last job first), the address of the company, salary, position, and reason for leaving

14. Students should list three adults not related to them and include full addresses and how long they have known each.

15. Students should list any major injuries or handicaps that may have an impact on their work performance.

16. Students should list a person who can be contacted in case of emergency and include the full address and phone number.

17. (There is no answer.)

18. today's date; name signed (not printed)

ACTIVITY 7—Filling Out Job Applications (p. 150)

The answers on the McDonald's form (pp. 151-152) and the general form (pp. 153-154) will vary. Students should print clearly and fill out the forms completely. It may be helpful to prepare a list of possible jobs for students to consider.

The McDonald's form includes a W–4 withholding allowance form that should be completed as fully as possible. Students probably will claim only one allowance on line 4, unless they are married or have dependent children. Students whose incomes are very low or who are full-time students may claim exemption from withholding.

Check Your Understanding of Job Application Forms (p. 155)

1. Answers will vary.

2. usually, the most recent

3. an employer who offers equal chances for employment to all applicants regardless of race, sex, creed, or national origin

4. church membership

5. a temporary or current address as opposed to a person's regular, long-term address

6. a necessary (legal) job requirement or qualification

7. you may lose your job without having been notified in advance; an employer reserves the right to fire you

8. race, sex, age, creed, national origin (any three of these)

9. Answers will vary. Students who are very concerned about neatness and showing that they can follow directions properly may request a new form. Students who believe they can correct the form neatly may choose not to request a new form.

10. personal information, employment desired, education, former employers, references (any three of these or similar responses)

SHOW WHAT YOU KNOW... About Job Application Forms (p. 155)

Answers will vary.

ACTIVITY 8—Preparing for a Job Interview (p. 157)

Answers will vary.

ACTIVITY 9—Preparing for a Job Interview (p. 157)

Answers will vary but may include some of the following:

1. **Like:** The applicant will be able to get to work easily and on time.
   Dislike: The interviewer may feel that the applicant is more interested in the location than in the position.

2. **Like:** The interviewer may appreciate the applicant's honesty.
   Dislike: The interviewer may wonder why the applicant couldn't get along with the former boss or how well the applicant will fit in.

3. **Like:** The interviewer may appreciate the applicant's honesty and willingness to work overtime on some days.
   Dislike: The interviewer may wonder about the applicant's priorities.

4. **Like:** The interviewer may appreciate the applicant's honesty or feel that an applicant who really needs a job would be a good candidate.
   Dislike: The interviewer may feel that the applicant is not focussed enough about what he or she wants to do and will not be dedicated to the job.

5. **Like:** Unless the interviewer is a tennis fan, he or she is not likely to be satisfied with this answer. However, if the position is not yet available, this might be an acceptable answer.
   Dislike: The interviewer may wonder about the applicant's priorities.

ACTIVITY 10—Preparing for a Job Interview (p. 158)

1. c

2. c

3. c

4. c

5. b

6. c

7. b

8. c

SHOW WHAT YOU KNOW... About Job Interviews (p. 161)

Role plays will vary.

Check Your Understanding of Job Interviews (p. 160)

1. F

2. T (for most jobs)

3. F

4. F

5. F

6. Answers will vary. The answer should focus on the applicant's desire for more growth, responsibility, or training, rather than on the conflict with the former boss.

7. Answers will vary. The answer should focus on the fact that regular transportation is available or has already been arranged.

8. Answers will vary. The answer should include an apology for the inconvenience of the delay and a promise that the applicant will not be late again.

9. Answers will vary. As in question 6, the answer should focus on the applicant's desire for growth, rather than on the conflict.

10. Answers will vary. The answer should be more specific than the example, explaining either why the applicant needs a job or why the applicant chose this company to apply to.

ACTIVITY 11—Telephoning about a Job (p. 164)

Ad #1

The first response is unsuitable. The ad clearly reads "Wanted—High School Students."

The second response is unsuitable. Although at first this response may appear to be suitable, a close reading of the ad will show that the applicant is free to request more information about the job over the phone. A specific question about the job would be more appropriate.

The third response is suitable. This is an appropriate response to "Call 555-7013 for information." The applicant does want more information and is requesting how to go about getting it.

Ad #2

The first response is suitable. The applicant waits until he or she reaches ext. 481 to ask for someone who would know something about the tutoring job. The applicant also identifies the paper where the ad appeared.

The second response is suitable. Although many employers will not discuss pay over the phone, this is a suitable question for this ad. Since the employer has not given a specific job location or the name of a person to contact, the applicant is justified in trying to get more information over the phone. The applicant was correct in waiting to reach ext. 481 with this question.

The third response is unsuitable. The ad specifically reads, "Nights." The employer is asking that each applicant screen himself or herself before calling.

The fourth response is unsuitable. The switchboard operator is the wrong person to ask.

The fifth response is suitable. This request is precise and concise. The applicant recognizes from the ad that 555-6130 is a switchboard. He or she must give an extension number.

ACTIVITY 12—Evaluating Telephone Interviews (p. 166)

Ad #1

1. Answers will vary.

2. The applicant achieved goal #1, but the applicant *did not* achieve goal #2. The employer merely wants to schedule interviews in advance. No salary information will be given out over the phone.

Ad #2

1. Answers will vary.

2. Yes, the applicant achieved her goal. She made the interviewer (Anne Hutchinson) aware of her qualifications and accepted the time suggested by the interviewer without hesitation.

ACTIVITY 13—Taking Phone Messages (p. 170)

IMPORTANT MESSAGE

FOR *Mr. Baker*
DATE *today's date*   TIME *9:40* A.M. ~~P.M.~~
M~~r~~. *Robert Whitney*
OF
PHONE _____ *555-0703* _____
        AREA CODE   NUMBER   EXTENSION

TELEPHONED	✓	PLEASE CALL	
CAME TO SEE YOU		WILL CALL AGAIN	✓
WANTS TO SEE YOU		RUSH	
RETURNED YOUR CALL		SPECIAL ATTENTION	

MESSAGE *He wants to discuss a case you are handling for him. Please call him tomorrow at home if he does not reach you today at 2 pm*
SIGNED *(Student's name)*
LITHO IN USA

TOPS ● FORM 3002P

IMPORTANT MESSAGE

FOR *John Penn*
DATE *today's date*   TIME *3:30* A.M. ~~P.M.~~
M~~r~~. *Arnold Jenkins*
OF *Whitney Electronics*
PHONE *304* - *252-0401*   *21*
        AREA CODE   NUMBER   EXTENSION

TELEPHONED	✓	PLEASE CALL	
CAME TO SEE YOU		WILL CALL AGAIN	
WANTS TO SEE YOU		RUSH	
RETURNED YOUR CALL		SPECIAL ATTENTION	

MESSAGE *He will have the information you requested tomorrow at 9 am*

SIGNED *J.J.*
LITHO IN USA

TOPS ● FORM 3002P

Check Your Understanding of Telephone Skills (p. 173)

Answers will vary but should include the information in the following example:

> To: David Jacobson
> From: Jim Brown's Bookstore, 555-4582
> Date: Today's Date
> Mr. Brown called. The book you ordered, *How to Write a Resume,* probably
> won't be in until January 1. Will call when book comes in.
> (Signature)

As worded, the memo could have also been a personal memo. Here is an example of
the message as a personal memo:

> David,
> Mr. Brown of Jim Brown's Bookstore called. *How To Write a Resume* probably
> won't be in until January 1. He will call when the book comes in. His telephone
> number is 555-4582.
> (Signed with a first name)

1–5 Answers will vary. Some examples:

1. "Mr. Greene is out of the office. May I help you?"

2. "Hello. I am calling about the part-time job at Burger Bar that was advertised in the
Tribune."

3. "Hello. This is (student's name). I am calling for Mr. Greene, of Northbrook
Computers. Mr. Greene would like to make an appointment with you on either
Monday or Tuesday morning of next week. Mr. Greene has told me that you are
expecting a call from him about the appointment."

4. "Hello. I am calling about the part-time warehouse job you have recently advertised. I need to know if after school hours are available."

5. Hello. I would like to inquire about a part-time job as a sales clerk. Will you please
tell me if you have any openings?"

SHOW WHAT YOU KNOW... About Telephone Skills (p. 174)

Role plays will vary.

CHAPTER 8
Filling Out Forms (p. 175)

Objectives

After completing this chapter the student will be able to:

1. Define and use vocabulary words related to various everyday forms.

2. Complete everyday forms correctly.

3. Correctly fill out bank checks and deposit slips.

4. Demonstrate two methods of filling out the "dollar line" of a personal check.

5. Make entries in a checkbook register.

6. Answer questions about bank statements.

7. Understand and complete charge card applications.

8. Complete an order form.

9. Complete income tax returns 1040EZ and 1040A.

Suggested Activities

1. In Activity 10, p. 193, a list of the abbreviations (codes) found most often on bank statements appeared on Anne Marie Ramos's statement. Discuss these terms and their meanings in class.

2. In "Show What You Know," p. 200, students are asked to bring two credit applications to class. These applications can be from local stores, banks, department stores, or gas stations. Below are discussion questions that can be used for this activity:

   • Does the application request the applicant's social security number?

   • Are there any questions pertaining to age, sex, or race? (These factors should not influence a creditor's decision to give credit. They will most likely not appear on a credit application. Discrimination based on age, sex, or race is illegal.)

- If there is space provided for information on a co-applicant, is that person's signature required?

- Sometimes there is a clause granting a creditor permission to investigate any of the credit information you have provided and holding you responsible for accurate, truthful information. Is such a clause on your application?

- In what form is salary information requested? . . . weekly? . . . biweekly? . . . monthly/net? . . . gross? . . . take-home?

- Are you required to list all your debts (outstanding obligations) or does the creditor specify a certain number of credit references?

3. If there are students in class who do not have social security cards, send them to the local social security office to apply.

4. Below you will find a list of forms that were not discussed in this chapter. Secure samples of these forms. Copy and distribute them for class discussion.

- money order

- rent (or other) written receipts

- change-of-address form

- application for an apartment

- unemployment application

ANSWERS

ACTIVITY 1—Understanding the Vocabulary of Everyday Forms (p. 176)

1. C

2. F

3. G

4. I

5. D

6. B

7. H

8. J

9. A

10. E

11. revoked/suspended

12. valid

13. in lieu of

14. naturalized

15. mandatory

ACTIVITY 2—Completing Forms (p. 178)
Library Card Applications/Request for Information

Answers will vary.

ACTIVITY 3—Voter Registration Forms (p. 179)

1. Lance Adam Patterson

2. vote

3. 803 Long Lake Road, Elizabeth (New Jersey); Union

4. new registration

5. Vaughn P. Jonas

ACTIVITY 4—Filling Out an Application for a
Social Security Card (p. 182)

1. T

2. T

3. F

4. T

5. T

Check Your Understanding of Forms (p. 184)

Answers will vary. The instructions for filling out the social security application are found on p. 181 of the student text. If students do not already have social security numbers, encourage them to complete an actual form, available at their local social security office.

SHOW WHAT YOU KNOW... About Forms (p. 184)

Answers will vary.

ACTIVITY 5—Filling in the "Dollars" Line (p. 187)

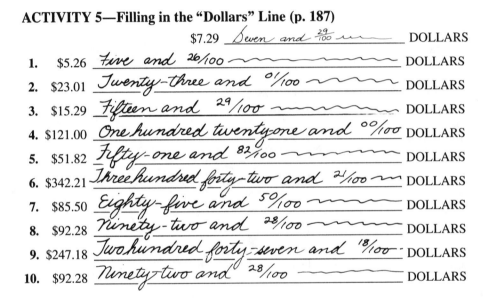

$7.29 _Seven and 29/100_ DOLLARS

1. $5.26 _Five and 26/100_ DOLLARS
2. $23.01 _Twenty-three and 01/100_ DOLLARS
3. $15.29 _Fifteen and 29/100_ DOLLARS
4. $121.00 _One hundred twenty-one and 00/100_ DOLLARS
5. $51.82 _Fifty-one and 82/100_ DOLLARS
6. $342.21 _Three hundred forty-two and 21/100_ DOLLARS
7. $85.50 _Eighty-five and 50/100_ DOLLARS
8. $92.28 _Ninety-two and 28/100_ DOLLARS
9. $247.18 _Two hundred forty-seven and 18/100_ DOLLARS
10. $92.28 _Ninety-two and 28/100_ DOLLARS

ACTIVITY 6—Writing Checks (p. 187)

1.

JAMES C. OR MARY A. MORRISON
1765 SHERIDAN DRIVE
YOUR CITY, STATE   12345

127

today's date 19 —   00-6789/0000

PAY TO THE ORDER OF *Payne's Department Store* $ *10.30*

Ten and 30/100   DOLLARS

THE BANK OF YOUR CITY
YOUR CITY, USA 12345

MEMO *payment*

Mary A. Morrison
SAMPLE VOID

⑈0000678941⑈ 12345678⑈

2.

JAMES C. OR MARY A. MORRISON
1765 SHERIDAN DRIVE
YOUR CITY, STATE   12345

128

today's date 19 —   00-6789/0000

PAY TO THE ORDER OF *Leed's Variety Store* $ *9.17*

Nine and 17/100   DOLLARS

THE BANK OF YOUR CITY
YOUR CITY, USA 12345

MEMO *art supplies*

Mary A. Morrison
SAMPLE VOID

⑈0000678941⑈ 12345678⑈

3.

JAMES C. OR MARY A. MORRISON
1765 SHERIDAN DRIVE
YOUR CITY, STATE   12345

129

today's date 19 —   00-6789/0000

PAY TO THE ORDER OF *Appalachian Power Company* $ *29.00*

Twenty-nine and 00/100   DOLLARS

THE BANK OF YOUR CITY
YOUR CITY, USA 12345

MEMO *electric bill* 853-470

Mary A. Morrison
SAMPLE VOID

⑈0000678941⑈ 12345678⑈

(Note: Students also may sign checks "James C. Morrison.")

ACTIVITY 7—Filling Out a Deposit Slip (p. 189)

1. $10

2. September 15, 1994

3. no

4. two; $101.38; $10.00

5. 1-234-5678

ACTIVITY 8—Keeping a Checkbook Register (p. 191)

1. $500

2. Montgomery Ward

3. July 16

4. a scarf

5. $440

6. Dr. Altchek

7. $387.50

8. August 14

9. $370

10. 868

ACTIVITY 9—Keeping a Checkbook Register (p. 192)

		RECORD ALL CHARGES OR CREDITS THAT AFFECT YOUR ACCOUNT					BALANCE	
NUMBER	DATE	DESCRIPTION OF TRANSACTION	PAYMENT/DEBIT (-)	√ T	FEE IF ANY (-)	DEPOSIT/CREDIT (+)	300	00
201		Myrtle's Daycare	35 00				265	00
202		Zilm's Drugs	15 82				249	18
203		Jackson's Dept Store	21 00				228	18
204		Consumer's Power	46 82				181	36
205		Carson's Boutique	56 94				124	42
206		Ned's Place	48 52				75	90
		Cash Deposit				400 00	475	90

(Date column should show today's date for each check and deposit recorded.)

ACTIVITY 10—Reading a Monthly Statement (p. 193)

1. checks

2. July 15; August 14

3. $500

4. $460

5. checks

6. deposit

7. $50

8. 22

Check Your Understanding of Bank Forms (p. 194)

1. $3.49 *Three and 49/100*

2. $43.52 *Forty-three and 52/100*

3. $207.09 *Two hundred seven and 09/100*

4. $764.50 *Seven hundred sixty-four and 50/100*

5. $25.02 *Twenty-five and 02/100*

6. b

7. c

8. a

9. b

10. a

ACTIVITY 11—Filling Out An Application for a Credit Card (p. 197)

1. Charles E. Wright

2. two

3. yes

4. renting an apartment

5. yes; Harford Company

6. $2,500

7. $2,000

8. yes; yes; no

9. Frances Wright

10. Smith's Clothing

11. spouse of Charles Wright

12. teacher

13. yes

14. Answers will vary.

ACTIVITY 12—Completing Credit Card Applications (p. 198)

Information on applications will vary. All information except signature should be printed.

1. Student may check preferred title if desired.

2. name, first name first; age

3. address including ZIP Code; length of residence

4. check correct box; monthly rent or mortgage; social security number, phone number, and number of dependents

5. Student should print former address if he or she has lived at address in line 3 for less than two years.

6. employer's name, address including ZIP Code, and length of employment

7. Student should list previous employer if he or she has worked less than one year for current employer.

8. Student should list other income and source if desired.

9. bank name and address, type of account(s), and account number(s)

10. any previous Sears account information

11. names of others who will use account, if appropriate

12. up to three credit references

13. an adult personal reference other than spouse

14. sign name; today's date

ACTIVITY 13—Applying for a Loan (p. 200)

Information on application will vary.

ACTIVITY 14—Completing Order Forms (p. 202)

Answers will vary. Have students exchange forms and check each other's work.

ACTIVITY 15—Understanding Income Tax Words (p. 205)

If possible, have instruction booklets and forms for 1040EZ and 1040A available in the classroom so students can practice filling out their own returns.

  1. D

  2. I

  3. A

  4. J

  5. C

  6. F

  7. E

  8. G

  9. H

10. B

ACTIVITY 16—Working with Income Tax Words (p. 205)

return; wages; interest; adjusted gross income; dependent; withheld; tax table; refund

ACTIVITY 17—Using a 1040EZ (p. 206)

1. yes

2. $2000

3. $50

4. yes

5. yes

6. line 8

ACTIVITY 18—Working with Income Tax Words (p. 210)

joint return; dependent; exemptions; interest; dividends; tax-exempt; unemployment compensation; IRA; withheld; refund

ACTIVITY 19—Using 1040A (p. 211)

1. yes

2. Married filing joint return (or 2)

3. yes

4. dependent son

5. 3

6. $48,899

7. $180

8. yes

9. line 9

10. yes

11. no

12. no

13. yes

14. that is the amount allowed for one exemption on 6e

15. $35,999

16. yes

17. 27

18. 28a

19. no

20. yes

Check Your Understanding of Tax Forms (p. 214)

(Numbers 1–8 below refer to line numbers on Form 1040EZ—1992—shown in the student text.)

Alexander	1.	2,350	
	2.	36	
	3.	2,386	
	4.	yes	2,350
	5.	36	
	6.	72	
	7.	6	
	8.	66	
Fletcher	1.	11,020	
	2.	380	
	3.	11,400	
	4.	5,900	
	5.	5,500	
	6.	975	
	7.	829	
	8.	146	

You may wish to have students work on blank 1040EZ forms available at your local IRS office, complete with the worksheet on the back.

CHAPTER 9

Reference Strategies (p. 216)

Objectives

After completing this chapter the student will be able to:

1. Locate books in a library using the card catalog.

2. Locate books in a library using the computer.

3. Use alphabetizing skills to locate books on library shelves.

4. Identify the call number group for books on various subjects.

5. Use the *Readers' Guide to Periodical Literature* to find articles on specific topics.

6. Use guide words and alphabetizing skills to locate various words in a dictionary.

7. Understand how to use a dictionary pronunciation key.

8. Understand the parts of a dictionary entry.

9. Use tables of contents to locate information in books and magazines.

10. Use a book index to identify the page or pages that contain information on specific topics.

11. Use a merchandise catalog index to locate items within the catalog.

12. Locate the page or pages of specific business listings using the headings in a Yellow Pages index.

13. Define and use vocabulary words related to libraries, dictionaries, tables of contents, and indexes.

Suggested Activities

1. Plan a tour of your local library. Be sure students are familiar with the card catalog, the computer, the divisions of the library, and the library's system for classifying books. If any students do not have a library card, help them apply for one.

2. Divide the class into teams. Secure two copies each of various indexes and tables of contents. Take these from drivers' training manuals, catalogs, car owner's manuals, or popular trade magazines. Make a list of topics to find and questions to answer. Students from each team can compete to quickly identify the page containing the requested information.

ANSWERS

ACTIVITY 1—Using the Card Catalog (p. 218)

1. Br-Ch

2. O-Pe

3. U-Z

4. Bi-Bo

5. Pe-Pi

6. Ri-So

7. Ch-D

8. A-Bei

9. Ri-So

10. Pe-Pi

11. Te-U

12. Ch-D

13. L

14. E-G

15. M

ACTIVITY 2—Using a Computer (p. 222)

1. Witch

2. Jane

3. Brontë

4. Austen

5. Old

6. Doyle

7. Kerr

8. Simon

9. Raisin

10. David

ACTIVITY 3—Using the Dewey Decimal System (p. 224)

1. 800–899

2. 100–199

3. 800–899

4. 700–799

5. 500–599

6. 500–599

7. 900–999

8. 600–699

9. 200–299

10. 400–499

ACTIVITY 4—Using the *Readers' Guide* (p. 227)

1. Any two of the following: Beatles, Chipmunks, Disco groups, records—Rock music, Rock musicians

2. Abba: Ready for the Fortune 500

3. Hi Fi (*High Fidelity*)

4. *Teen*

5. Nov. 27, 1980

6. Chipmunks (recording group)

7. J. Farber; yes

8. November and December

9. 13

10. yes

Check Your Understanding of Reference Strategies (p. 228)

1. T

2. T

3. T

4. T

5. T

6. F

7. F

8. T

9. F

10. F

SHOW WHAT YOU KNOW... About Reference Works (p. 228)

Answers will vary. Students should be encouraged to become familiar with using the almanac, gazetteer, and world atlas.

ACTIVITY 5—Locating Words in a Dictionary (p. 230)

compete

competency

competitive

complacence

complacency

complex

point

position

posse

possess

possessed

postage

ACTIVITY 6—Using Guide Words (p. 232)

hilt/hold	holder/hooky	hooligan/houseboat
history	homework	horoscope
hogwash	honey	hostage
hoax	honest	hotshot
hives	hole	horror
hint	homage	hospital

ACTIVITY 7—Using the Pronunciation Key (p. 234)

Answers will vary.

ACTIVITY 8—Using the Pronunciation Key and Accent Marks (p. 235)

1. cinema

2. classical

3. complication

4. encyclopedia

5. Florida

6. Houston

7. jaw

8. joy

9. bilingual

10. thyme

11. though

12. whim

SHOW WHAT YOU KNOW... About the Pronunciation Key and Accent Marks (p. 235)

Because he put on his turn signal every time he made a turn.

ACTIVITY 9—Understanding Dictionary Entries (p. 237)

1. sardonically

2. noun

3. yes

4. yes

5. sarongs

6. two

7. no

8. 1

ACTIVITY 10—Understanding Dictionary Entries (p. 237)

1. Japanese

2. His clothes were a sartorial triumph.

3. Informal

4. after the second syllable

5. American Indian

6. Bigfoot

7. Yes

ACTIVITY 11—Understanding Dictionary Entries (p. 239)

1. 1856

2. William

3. Atlantic

4. 705 B.C.

5. Regina

ACTIVITY 12—Using the Dictionary to Check Spelling (p. 240)

1. recommend

2. accommodate

3. accumulate

4. occasion

5. personnel

6. benefit

7. ninth

8. vacuum

9. omitted

10. occurred

11. committee

12. valuable

13. separate

14. arrangement

Check Your Understanding of Dictionaries (p. 241)

1. cow

2. noun

3. 2; 4

4. be too polite or slavish

5. after the second syllable

6. Colonel James Bowie

7. at the entrance to Manila Bay, Philippines

8. an Italian painter

9. no, it's a city in Texas

10. bowmen

SHOW WHAT YOU KNOW... About Dictionaries (p. 242)

Answers will vary. Students should be encouraged to use their imaginations in coining new words and meanings.

ACTIVITY 13—Using the Table of Contents of a Book (p. 245)

1. four

2. Courage Was Their Companion; "I Have a Dream"

3. 12; 11

4. 66; 118

5. a poet

6. Isaac Asimov

ACTIVITY 14—Using the Table of Contents of a Magazine (p. 246)

1. order in which the articles appear

2. a. every month

    b. every month

    c. this month

    d. this month

    e. this month

3. 451

4. 78

5. 4

Check Your Understanding of Contents Pages (p. 248)

  1. Section 1 and Section 2

  2. Using Vivid Words; Nouns and Verbs; Adjectives and Adverbs; Intensifiers

  3. 28

  4. Personal Writing: Writing for Yourself

  5. two

  6. Planning Your Life Story

  7. Chapter 7

  8. Let's Write!

  9. six

  10. four

ACTIVITY 15—Using a Book Index (p. 251)

1. 237–239

2. 21

3. three

4. 89–91

5. 39–42; 36–38; 43–45

ACTIVITY 16—Using a Catalog Index (p. 252)

"Find-it-Fast Index"

 1. 154–174

 2. 103–126

 3. 80–93

 4. 175–179

 5. 4–79

 6. 241–252

Main Index

 7. 168

 8. 160

 9. 103

10. 173

11. 190, 191

12. 143, 224

13. back cover

14. 133, 134, 137, 158

15. 118

16. 167

17. 216–218, 250

18. 209

19. 235

20. 155

Check Your Understanding of Indexes (p. 254)

  1. 34

  2. 31

  3. 33

  4. 28

  5. 3 (or 5)

  6. 16

  7. 20

  8. 20

  9. 12 (Both "Barbers" and "Beauty Salons" are on p. 12.)

10. 18

CHAPTER 10

Using Directories and Floor Plans (p. 256)

Objectives

After completing this chapter the student will be able to:

1. Identify the floor location of specific items by using a store directory.

2. Identify the locations of various store departments using a floor directory.

3. Answer questions about information found in a building directory.

4. Locate specific points on a floor plan.

5. Locate telephone numbers in the white and yellow pages of the telephone book.

6. Use the yellow pages to locate specific information about businesses.

7. Find area codes for specific geographical areas using an area code map.

8. Define and use vocabulary words related to directories, floor plans, and telephone books.

Suggested Activities

1. Local government agencies usually are listed in the white pages of the telephone book. Many telephone directories also carry special blue pages listing county, state, and federal agencies. In Activity 10 (p. 268), an important agency is listed: the Poison Control Center. Knowing how to locate government agencies is a necessary resource skill. It should be discussed in conjunction with the telephone book. Secure sufficient copies of local directories to give all students practice in finding city, state, and county listings.

2. Familiarize students with the emergency telephone numbers found in the front cover of the telephone book. These numbers should include the police department, the fire department, and the rescue squad. The general emergency number in most urban areas is "911." Operators are also trained to handle emergency telephone calls. An operator can be reached simply by dialing "0" and saying, "Operator, this is an emergency . . . ." Find out if there is a local number for a Poison Control

Center. In some areas there is an 800 (toll free) number for the nearest Poison Control Center and an 800 number for reporting polluting toxic chemicals and oil spills.

ANSWERS

ACTIVITY 1—Using Store Directories (p. 257)

1. 3

2. 1

3. 2

4. 2

5. 2

6. 2

7. 1

8. 1

9. 2

10. 3

11. 2

12. 3

13. 2

14. 2

15. 1

16. 1

17. 1

18. 2

19. 3

20. 3

21. 1

22. 3

23. 2

24. 1

25. 1 or (3)

26. 2

27. 1

28. 1

29. 2

30. 1

ACTIVITY 2—Using a Floor Directory for a Department Store (p. 258)

1. seventh

2. fifth

3. second if you are female; third if you are male

4. third

5. fourth

6. fifth

7. sixth

8. fourth

9. seventh

10. seventh

ACTIVITY 3—Using Building Directories (p. 259)

1. 10; 10

2. 10

3. no

4. yes

5. 10

6. yes

7. Martin Wholesalers

8. Marvel Photos

9. one

10. one

11. 6

12. a. 708

    b. 502

    c. 611

    d. 613

    e. 707

    f. 605

    g. 1013

    h. 510

ACTIVITY 4—Using Floor Plans (p. 261)

1. West

2. two

3. yes

4. yes

5. east and north

6. ten

7. no

8. yes

Check Your Understanding of Directories and Floor Plans (p. 262)

1. alphabetically

2. left

3. right

4. mezzanine

5. Daisy's Donut Shop, A–1

6. Norge's Portraits, B–2

ACTIVITY 5—Reading the White Pages (p. 264)

1. 555-8332

2. 555-4149

3. 555-8866

4. 555-3321

5. 555-7899

6. 555-8254

ACTIVITY 6—Locating Telephone Numbers for Persons with the Same Names (p. 264)

1. 555-2813

2. 555-3245

3. 555-6471

4. three

5. 555-7110

6. 555-3331

ACTIVITY 7—Deciding When to Use the Yellow Pages (p. 265)

1. Answers will vary but may include: easy to locate all businesses offering the service, product, or specialty you are looking for; easy to find store that is most conveniently located; may be able to find out hours; may be able to get directions; may be able to call ahead and check if item is available.

2. yellow pages

3. white pages (Since you already know the name of the shop, the white pages should be faster.)

ACTIVITY 8—Classifying Yellow-Page Listings (p. 266)

Furniture Listings

1. c

2. c

3. a

4. b

5. b

6. a (sometimes b)

7. a

8. b

9. c

10. a

Car Businesses

1. d

2. d

3. b

4. b

5. d

6. d

7. a

8. d

9. d

10. a

11. c

12. e

13. c

14. a

15. e

16. c

ACTIVITY 9—Reading and Understanding the Yellow Pages (p. 267)

1. dry cleaners

2. DeLuxe Dry Cleaners Plant

3. Sudden Service Cleaners

4. yes (heading says *Cleaners—Cont'd.*)

5. a service

6. Phyl's One Hour Martinizing

7. Mr. Suds Dry Cleaning; Querbach Leather Process Inc.; Suburban Dry Cleaners & Shirt Launderers

8. Guida Dry Cleaners

9. Realgood Cleaners

ACTIVITY 10— Choosing the Yellow Pages or the White Pages (p. 268)

1. a

2. c

3. c

4. a

5. c

6. a

7. c

8. b

9. a

10. b

11. c

12. c

13. a

14. c

15. a

16. b

17. c

18. c

19. c

20. c

ACTIVITY 11—Reading Area Code Maps (p. 268)

1. Arizona, 602; South Dakota, 605; Wyoming, 307; Utah, 801

2. Alaska, 907; Hawaii, 808; Bermuda, 809; Puerto Rico, 809

3. Ontario Canada, 807, 705, 519, 416, 613; Quebec, 819, 418, 514; Saskatchewan, 306

4. Florida—four (904, 407, 305, 813); West Virginia—one (304); Georgia—three (404, 706, 912); Montana—one (406); Texas—eight (806, 817, 915, 214, 903, 713, 409, 512)

5. San Antonio (512); Houston (713); Dallas (214)

6. 215

7. 404

ACTIVITY 12—Reading Area Code Maps (p. 270)

Situation #1

A. Mr. Brown just left for lunch. New York time: 12:01 P.M.

Situation #2

C. Call back in an hour. Des Moines time: 2:00 P.M.

Check Your Understanding of Telephone Directories (p. 271)

1. S

2. Carpenters

3. Bus lines

4. look under Plumbing; Plumbers; or Plumbing & Heating.

5. P (or Pierce)

6. 10:30 A.M.

7. b

8. MacDonald; Mack; Major; McKay; McNeil; Miner

9. Avenue

10. one home number and one office number

CHAPTER 11
Special Reading Strategies (p. 272)

Objectives

After completing this chapter the student will be able to:

1. Identify street and highway signs.

2. Locate specific places on a trail, street, and highway map.

3. Understand a map legend.

4. Locate specific information on bus, train, and plane schedules.

5. Determine if a timetable should be read across, down, or up and down.

6. Answer questions about information found in various charts.

7. Answer questions based on information from line, bar, and circle graphs.

8. Define and use vocabulary words related to maps, charts, graphs, and time tables.

Suggested Activities

1. Students should list and/or draw various signs not mentioned in this chapter. They should recall symbols for men's and women's rest rooms, "no smoking" signs, and signs for facilities to be used by the physically challenged. Often, signs consist of symbols only.

2. Your local chamber of commerce or city government offices are a good source for securing city maps. State offices of transportation or tourism can provide state highway maps. Have students study these maps in class. Students should be able to locate and use the street or town index and map key, locate public buildings and points of interest, find where they live, and point to the school's location.

3. Provide as many different types of maps as possible in the classroom: atlases, historic maps, world maps, maps of foreign cities, topographical maps, county maps, and so on. Mention that drawings showing waterways and harbors are called charts. If you live near a charted waterway, your local library may have a chart of the area. If not, a librarian can tell you where to write for one.

4. Discuss the occupations that involve making and using maps. Define the words *cartographer* and *cartography* and mention that maps are important to travel agents, bus drivers, and over-the-road truck drivers.

5. Assign small groups to complete the following activity using a highway map of the United States and a mileage chart.

   As tour director for a travel planner, you must map out a tour from Minneapolis to Chicago to St. Louis and back to Minneapolis. The tour is to leave early Monday morning. What routes should the tour take to assure that travelers have at least two *full* days in Chicago and two days in St. Louis? When will the tour arrive back in Minneapolis? Prepare a daily schedule beginning Monday morning. Assume that the bus travels an average of sixty miles an hour.

   Key: Minneapolis to Chicago distance is approximately 410 miles; at 60 mph this takes 7 hours.

   Chicago to St. Louis distance is approximately 289 miles; at 60 mph this takes 4½–5 hours.

   St. Louis to Minneapolis distance is approximately 630 miles; at 60 mph this takes 10 hours.

   Suggested schedule:

Leave Monday at 7 A.M.	Arr. Chicago 2 P.M.
Tuesday	Chicago
Wednesday	Chicago
Leave Chicago Thursday at 7 A.M.	Arr. St. Louis noon
Friday	St. Louis
Saturday	St. Louis
Leave St. Louis Sunday at 8 A.M.	Arr. Minneapolis 6 P.M.

ANSWERS

ACTIVITY 1—Identifying Regulatory Signs (p. 275)

1. C

2. A

3. E

4. H

5. B

6. F

7. D

8. G

9. I

10. J

ACTIVITY 2—Identifying Warning Signs (p. 278)

1. G

2. D

3. H

4. F

5. B

6. I

7. C

8. A

9. K

10. E

ACTIVITY 3—Identifying Street and Highway Signs (p. 280)

1st row: regulatory, regulatory, service and guide

2nd row: warning, warning, service and guide

Check Your Understanding of Street and Highway Signs (p. 281)

1. No U turn

2. Curve ahead

3. Intersection—watch for cars crossing, entering, or leaving highway

4. Picnic table

5. No right turn

6. Watch for schoolchildren

7. No trucks

8. A bridge or underpass ahead; clearance is 12 feet, 6 inches

9. Hill—drivers must take special care

10. Traffic may be moving into your lane; be ready to change your speed or lane.

SHOW WHAT YOU KNOW... About Street and Highway Signs (p. 282)

Groups' signs will vary.

ACTIVITY 4—Understanding a Trail Map (p. 285)

1. 5 miles

2. Difficult and Moderate

3. Moderate

4. yes

5. one

6. west

7. back

8. left

ACTIVITY 5—Understanding a Map Legend (p. 286)

1. state highway

2. railroad

3. interstate route

4. state park

5. freeway or tollway (Note: On a four-color map, the symbol for freeway is in one color and the symbol for tollway is in another.)

6. U.S. route number

7. airport

8. county seat

9. state trail

10. state tourist information center

ACTIVITY 6—Understanding a Street Map (p. 288)

1. Woodward

2. Municipal Courts

3. Wayne County Community College

4. yes

5. interstate highway

6. six; five

7. east/west

8. no

ACTIVITY 7—Finding Locations with an Index and Grid (p. 291)

1. south

2. Olive

3. two

4. B–3

5. one

6. southeast

7. left

8. left

9. Take Lime north to Alhambra and turn west, or take San Miguel west to Plum and go north to Alhambra and turn east.

10. El Camino, Canyon, and Rodeo

ACTIVITY 8—Understanding a State Highway Map (p. 292)

1. 94

2. 18

3. Big Foot Beach and Bong Recreation Area

4. Kettle Moraine State Forest

5. yes

6. yes

7. yes

8. Orfordville; Magnolia

9. smaller

10. yes

Check Your Understanding of Maps (p. 293)

1. 83

2. 95

3. 895 (Harob Tunnel) or 695 (Francis Scott Key Bridge)

4. southeast

5. 695

6. Patapsco Valley State Park

7. Take Route 1 north to Route 40 east into Baltimore.

8. Major routes only are shown.

SHOW WHAT YOU KNOW... About Mapping a Route (p. 294)

Answers will vary.

ACTIVITY 9—Understanding Timetables (p. 297)

1. eight

2. 372 miles or 599 kilometers

3. 63

4. The Niagara Rainbow

5. 8:40 A.M.

6. 11:30 P.M.

7. Albany-Rensselaer

8. 11:27 A.M.

9. 4:40 P.M.

10. evening

ACTIVITY 10—Understanding Timetables (p. 298)

1. Augusta: 88/918; 4:25 P.M.; 6:25 P.M.; 1.
Charleston: 60; 8:10 A.M.; 8:52 A.M.; 0.
Columbia: 88/918; 4:25 P.M.; 7:01 P.M.; 2.

2. Atlanta: 5; Chicago: 3; Columbus: 1.

3. #943

4. Atlanta

5. #951

6. Atlanta; Charleston; Charlotte; Fayetteville/Fort Bragg; Greenville/Spartanburg; Hickory/Lenoir/Morganton; Knoxville/Oak Ridge (any four)

7. Saturdays

8. #24/927

ACTIVITY 11—Reading an Airport Terminal Schedule (p. 300)

1. 3:10; yes

2. 3:00; no

3. Flight #49; Flight #74; Flight #39

4. no; the plane is landing

5. 4:15; no

6. no

7. yes; 33

8. #412

9. Detroit

ACTIVITY 12—Understanding Timetables (p. 301)

1. Philadelphia and Ocean City

2. down

3. up

4. 10:05

5. 6:05; 6:35

6. 6:50; 8:25; 8:40

7. State Road, DE

8. 1st stop: Salisbury; 2nd stop: Milford; 3rd stop: Harrington; 4th stop: Dover; 5th stop: Smyrna

9. 3:35

10. 7:05

Check Your Understanding of Timetables (p. 303)

Down:	**1.**	The Pioneer
	2.	25; 26
	3.	11:25 P
	4.	12:20 A
	5.	12:35 A
	6.	11:10 A; 1:30 P; 6:00 P; 6:21 P
	7.	9:50 P
Up:	**1.**	7:10 A
	2.	Tacoma
	3.	11:00 A
	4.	11:10 A
	5.	Ontario
	6.	7:10 A

SHOW WHAT YOU KNOW... About Timetables (p. 304)

The train takes 22 hours to go 1081 miles. Average speed is 49 mph.

ACTIVITY 13—Reading a Temperature Chart (p. 306)

1. 54

2. 36

3. 93

4. December

5. August

6. Florence, SC

7. Asheville, NC

8. Savannah, GA

ACTIVITY 14—Reading a Recreation Site Chart (p. 307)

1. across

2. down

3. no

4. Beach Fork, Bluestone, Hawks Nest, Pricketts Fort, Tygart Lake

5. Blackwater Falls, Cacapon, Tygart Lake

6. the letter *N*

ACTIVITY 15—Reading a Line Graph (p. 309)

1. the track team

2. the cheerleaders

3. 65

4. 68

5. the track team

6. the cheerleaders

ACTIVITY 16—Reading a Bar Graph (p. 310)

1. 300

2. 200

3. 31–35

4. 500

5. 31–35

6. 17–20 and 26–30 age groups

7. 500

8. women

ACTIVITY 17—Reading a Circle Graph (p. 311)

1. c

2. a

3. d

4. b

5. d

Check Your Understanding of Graphs (p. 312)

1. 25%

2. married couple without children

3. over 50%

4. 40.3%

5. between 1970 and 1980

SHOW WHAT YOU KNOW... About Charts and Graphs (p. 313)

Answers should show understanding of a bar graph.

CHAPTER 12
Writing Workshop (p. 314)

Objectives

After completing this chapter the student will be able to:

1. Understand basic sentence patterns.

2. Understand and identify basic sentence parts.

3. Recognize kinds of sentences.

4. Recognize and revise fragments and run-on sentences.

5. Use correct verb forms and tenses.

6. Analyze and write topic and support sentences.

7. Write conclusions.

8. Edit and revise for punctuation, capitalization, and spelling.

9. Write letters to the editor, instructions, and memos.

Suggested Activities

1. Much advertising and other published matter are incorrect in matters of grammar, usage, spelling, and mechanics. As you work through this unit, collect and have students collect and analyze ads and other writing in newspapers, magazines, signs, brochures, menus, and catalogs.

2. Encourage students to analyze each other's writing as often as possible. Model supportive criticism of students' writing efforts, and emphasize that the goal is to discuss and analyze the writing, not the writer. No remarks directed toward a writer should be allowed; comments should begin with statements such as these: "This piece of writing is . . . ;" "This paragraph is . . . ;" or "These ideas are . . . "

3. If possible, invite several people to speak to the class about the writing they do on the job. Secretaries, hospital personnel, small-business owners, department managers in large businesses, social workers, editors, and restaurant and cafeteria

managers, for example, will have varied and interesting insights into writing at work and writing with a word processor.

4. A student having severe problems expressing herself or himself in writing may be helped by having you, an aide, or a tutor write while the student dictates. The student is then helped to see how what is said is transferred to paper or a word processor, how to revise dictated writings, and how to begin to write without this help.

5. Most students take quickly to writing with a word processor. With minor alterations in directions, most of the exercises in this chapter, except fill-in-the-blanks, can be completed on a word processor.

6. If your students are not already keeping journals, encourage them to do so. Journals help provide topics for writing, can help to stretch the imagination beyond television, and can help increase vocabulary. You might start by making regular journal assignments at first. *The English Journal* and "Notes Plus" often contain good ideas for fledgling student writers. Both are published by the National Council of Teachers of English.

ANSWERS

ACTIVITY 1—Using Basic Sentence Patterns (p. 318)

Added verbs will vary. Some suggestions for past-tense verbs follow, although students may add verbs in the present tense.

1. sat

2. ran/ate/spoke

3. spoke/sang

4. fixed/cooked

5. watched

6. played/dusted

7. found/wore/made

8. drew/showed

9. drank/bought/poured

10. read/wrote

ACTIVITY 2—Using Subjects (p. 318)

Added subjects will vary. Verbs to be underlined follow.

1. blew

2. swam

3. delivered

4. scrubbed

5. found

6. contributed

7. fought

8. sat

9. wrote

10. vote

ACTIVITY 3—Using Direct Objects (p. 319)

Answers will vary.

ACTIVITY 4—Using Indirect Objects (p. 320)

Answers will vary. Students may add nouns or pronouns as indirect objects.

ACTIVITY 5—Using Complements (p. 320)

Added complements will vary. Linking verbs to be underlined follow.

1. felt

2. are

3. seems

4. will be

5. was

ACTIVITY 6—Using Modifiers (p. 322)

Added modifiers will vary. Some suggestions follow.

1. (any number)

2. back/front/side

3. little/big/older/younger; science fiction/scary/detective

4. old/new (any color or shape)

5. quickly/fast

ACTIVITY 7—Writing Sentences (p. 324)

Answers will vary.

ACTIVITY 8—Identifying Main and Dependent Clauses (p. 325)

The following items can stand alone and should have checks and periods: 3, 4, 7, 8, 9, 10, 12, 15.

ACTIVITY 9—Using Main and Dependent Clauses (p. 326)

Answers will vary. Suggestions are shown.

1. We were tired

2. We had no water

3. We had to stop

4. We didn't know

5. We all got wet

Check Your Understanding of Sentences (p. 326)

1. simple (shown)

2. complex

3. simple

4. compound

5. compound-complex

6. simple

7. compound

8. simple

9. complex

10. complex

For items 6–10, you may want to have students underline subjects with one line and verbs with two.

SHOW WHAT YOU KNOW... About Sentences (p. 327)

Answers will vary.

ACTIVITY 10—Revising Sentence Fragments (p. 329)

1. Of the boys who tried out for basketball, only three failed to make the team, partly because they were still too short.

2. Unfortunately, when we were already late, we were given the wrong directions.

3. The telephone rang four times while you were watching television. **OR** While you were watching television, the telephone rang four times.

4. We thought you would pick up the dry cleaning since you were going that way.

5. We discovered Amy was going to be out of town after we planned her surprise party!

6. The last runners arrived about four o'clock, some limping, some barely able to talk. **OR** The last runners arrived about four o'clock. Some were limping and some were barely able to talk.

7. People fled Europe in the nineteenth century for many reasons, such as famine and persecution.

8. Flea markets do not appeal to me, especially when they are out-of-doors in rainy weather; however, some people never miss one. (Students may start a new sentence with *However.*)

ACTIVITY 11—Revising Run-on Sentences (p. 331)

1. Tornadoes and flooding often follow hurricanes. They are often as destructive as hurricanes.

2. Answers will vary. Suggestion: Hurricanes frequently start in the West Indies. They hit a coastline with great force, but they eventually lose their force as they blow across land.

3. Hurricane winds revolve in a violent counterclockwise direction. As a hurricane moves, winds are often clocked at well over a hundred miles an hour.

4. Hurricanes are a fact of life for many U.S. coastal cities. The 1992 hurricane named Andrew was the most destructive ever known up to that time.

5. Hurricanes cannot be prevented; however, loss of life can be diminished when people leave homes and businesses in coastal areas and travel inland.

ACTIVITY 12—Using Verb Tenses (p. 333)

You may want to discuss collective nouns such as *group, team, audience,* and *contents,* which take either singular or plural verbs, depending on meaning.

1. am

2. is

3. likes

4. buys

5. takes

6. call

7. stay

8. Were

9. Was

10. were

11. is

12. looks

13. tries

14. wishes

15. works

ACTIVITY 13—Using Verb Tenses (p. 336)

1. begun

2. wrote

3. seen

4. went

5. gone

6. eaten

7. gave

8. given

9. run

10. threw

11. burst

12. knew

13. written

14. drew

15. taken

ACTIVITY 14—Correcting Tense Shifts (p. 337)

1. and got out at my apartment.

2. but he came in anyway.

3. and then she had the students fill in the details.

4. he really studied the part.

5. gave us a few instructions.

Check Your Understanding of Tense and Subject-Verb Agreement (p. 338)

1. related

2. likes

3. amuses

4. took

5. chose

6. went

7. is

8. was

9. sews

10. bought

11. bake

12. want

ACTIVITY 15—Analyzing Topic Sentences (p. 341)

1. *Topic:* the day I disobeyed my father; *Attitude:* regret

2. *Topic:* my bedroom; *Attitude:* messiest room in our house

3. *Topic:* everyone attending last night's game; *Attitude:* physically and emotionally drained

4. *Topic:* real friendship; *Attitude:* value

ACTIVITY 16—Writing Better Topic Sentences (p. 341)

Answers will vary.

Sticking to the topic (p. 342)

Students should draw a line through the following sentences:

Paragraph 1.   Martha Washington died in 1802.

Paragraph 2.   We live at 1253 Linden Street.

Paragraph 3.   Cardigan sweaters are still worn today.

ACTIVITY 17—Writing Support Sentences (p. 344)

Answers will vary.

ACTIVITY 18—Evaluating Writing (p. 345)

1. Sugar is bad for your health.

2. the effect of sugar on health

3. yes   The writer tries to show through examples how sugar can be bad   for a person's health. The writer only discusses the effects of *sugar* in a diet.

4. yes

5. too much sugar in your diet can affect your health

ACTIVITY 19—Choosing a Closing Sentence (p. 346)

1. c (This sentence summarizes why Mrs. Marlow is respected and repeats the theme of the topic sentence.)

2. c (This sentence begins with a transition word to point out that it is a concluding statement.)

3. c (This sentence concludes the topic by taking a position based on the topic sentence. If this is true, then. . . .)

ACTIVITY 20—Using End Marks and Commas (p. 348)

1. Jane, please come home with us.

2. Do you like playing soccer?

3. Watch out!

4. I bought hamburgers, potato chips, and soft drinks.

5. Joe likes football, but he dislikes baseball.

6. Although sports programs for girls are new in some schools, the teams have done well.

7. Because it was raining, the game was canceled.

8. No, I don't like jogging.

9. Tina likes her new job, but the hours are too long.

10. M*A*S*H was on TV for eleven years, and the reruns will be on for a few more years.

ACTIVITY 21—Using Capital Letters (p. 350)

1. I really enjoyed the book *All Creatures Great and Small.*

2. My Aunt Ruth took me to a French restaurant with my cousins.

3. Is Austin a large city?

4. I always enjoy our family picnic at Greenland National Park.

5. Alex has a job at Bob's Big Burger on Elm Street.

ACTIVITY 22—Selecting the Right Word (p. 353)

1. counsel

2. principal

3. dessert

4. passed

5. lose

6. to

7. Who's

8. stationary

9. capital

10. It's

11. accept

12. altogether

13. all right

14. They're

15. there

16. piece

17. led

18. already

19. too

20. you're

ACTIVITY 23—Writing a Letter to the Editor (p. 357)

Look for evidence that students have supported their opinion and not simply repeated their opinion.

ACTIVITY 24—Writing Instructions (p. 358)

Students may or may not number their instructions. Instructions need not be in chronological order. Look for evidence that the student has thought through what the recipient of the instructions will need to be told. Students might evaluate each others' work and be encouraged to ask questions about unclear instructions.

ACTIVITY 25—Editing a Memo (p. 360)

For security reasons ~~and to prevent unauthorized people from entering and leaving the building~~, the Adams and Franklin doors will be locked at 5 p.m. ~~in the evening~~ every day~~, seven days a week~~. Employees and vendors may enter and exit only at the Maple Street entrance after 5 p.m. ~~Before 5 p.m., any entrance may be used.~~ We are sorry for any inconvenience this may cause~~, but we are doing it for security reasons~~.

ACTIVITY 26—Rewriting a Memo (p. 360)

Students should rewrite the memo to include a phone number for volunteers to call, location of Mason Park, and date of the fish fry.

ACTIVITY 27—Writing a Memo (p. 361)

Students having difficulty with this topic might assume other roles; for example, dance instructor, band leader, choir director, teacher, or scout leader.

Check Your Understanding of Sentences, Paragraphs, Punctuation, and Capitalization (p. 362)

Fifteen corrections are noted below.

Your chairperson met with members of the Mill Street Community Organization last week to discuss complaints about the Mill Street Art Fair in prevous years. *[1: i]*

Most of the complaints were about excessive noise, illegal parking, and inadequate clean-up. *[2]* ~~at the end of the weekend~~ *[3]* ~~on Sunday night~~ I feel that most complaints ~~was~~ *[4: were]* justified *[5a]* ~~A~~nd *[6]* that we have to be better ~~m~~ill Street nieghbors. *[7: M]* *[8: ei]*

I beleive *[9: ie]* that we can solve the noise and clean-up problems, but I'm not certain *[10]* how to deal with illegal parking. ~~B~~y closing the fair at 6 p.m. in the evening and *[11]* asking for more volunteers to help clean up, We might also ban street musicions *[12]* *[13: a]* entirely, preventing illegal parking may require more creative solutions. *[14]* *[15]*

Please plan to meet at my home, 22 E. Mill Street, on May 9 at 7 to discuss these complaints.

Select Bibliography

Baugh, L. Sue. *How to Write First-Class Letters.* Lincolnwood, IL: NTC Publishing Group, 1994.

Bowen, J. Donald, Madsen, Harold, and Hilferty, Ann. *TESOL Techniques and Procedures.* Rowley, MA: Newbury House, 1985.

Celce-Murcia, Marianne, and Larsen-Freeman, Diane. *The Grammar Book: An ESL/EFL Teacher's Course.* Rowley, MA: Newbury House, 1983.

Croft, Kenneth, ed. *Readings on English as a Second Language: For Teachers and Teacher Trainees.* Boston: Little, Brown, 1982.

Finocchiaro, Mary. *The Functional-Notional Approach: From Theory to Practice.* New York: Oxford, 1983.

Friedenberg, Joan E., and Bradley, Curtis H. *Finding a Job in the United States.* Lincolnwood, IL: National Textbook Company, 1986.

Friedenberg, Joan E., and Bradley, Curtis H. *The Vocational ESL Handbook.* Rowley, MA: Newbury House, 1984.

Kleinmann, Howard H., and Weissman, Julie. *Everyday Consumer English.* Lincolnwood, IL: National Textbook Company, 1985.

Maclin, Alice. *Reference Guide to English: A Handbook of English as a Second Language.* New York: Holt, Rinehart & Winston, 1987.

Maculaitis-Cooke, Jean, and Mona Scheraga. *The Complete ESL/EFL Resource Book.* Lincolnwood, IL: National Textbook Company, 1988.

Reynolds, Jerry D., Steet, Marion L., and Guillory, Ivory. *What You Need to Know About Improving Basic English Skills.* Lincolnwood, IL: National Textbook Company, 1992.

Rogers, Louisa. *Book of Forms for Everyday Living.* Lincolnwood, IL: National Textbook Company, 1989.

NTC LANGUAGE ARTS BOOKS

Business Communication
Handbook for Business Writing, *Baugh, Fryar, &*
Thomas
Meetings: Rules & Procedures, *Pohl*

Dictionaries
British/American Language Dictionary, *Moss*
NTC's Classical Dictionary, *Room*
NTC's Dictionary of Changes in Meaning, *Room*
NTC's Dictionary of Debate, *Hanson*
NTC's Dictionary of Literary Terms, *Morner &*
Rausch
NTC's Dictionary of Theatre and Drama Terms,
Mobley
NTC's Dictionary of Word Origins, *Room*
NTC's Spell It Right Dictionary, *Downing*
Robin Hyman's Dictionary of Quotations

Essential Skills
Building Real Life English Skills, *Starkey & Penn*
Developing Creative & Critical Thinking, *Boostrom*
English Survival Series, *Maggs*
Essential Life Skills, *Starkey & Penn*
Essentials of English Grammar, *Baugh*
Essentials of Reading and Writing English Series
Grammar for Use, *Hall*
Grammar Step-by-Step, *Pratt*
Guide to Better English Spelling, *Furness*
How to Be a Rapid Reader, *Redway*
How to Improve Your Study Skills, *Coman & Heavers*
How to Write Term Papers and Reports, *Baugh*
NTC Skill Builders
Reading by Doing, *Simmons & Palmer*
303 Dumb Spelling Mistakes, *Downing*
TIME: We the People, *ed. Schinke-Llano*
Vocabulary by Doing, *Beckert*

Genre Literature
Coming of Age, *Emra*
The Detective Story, *Schwartz*
The Short Story & You, *Simmons & Stern*
Sports in Literature, *Emra*
You and Science Fiction, *Hollister*

Journalism
Getting Started in Journalism, *Harkrider*
Journalism Today! *Ferguson & Patten*
Publishing the Literary Magazine, *Klaiman*
UPI Stylebook, *United Press International*

Language, Literature, and Composition
African American Literature, *Worley & Perry*
An Anthology for Young Writers, *Meredith*
The Art of Composition, *Meredith*
Creative Writing, *Mueller & Reynolds*
Handbook for Practical Letter Writing, *Baugh*
How to Write Term Papers and Reports, *Baugh*

In a New Land, *Grossman & Schur*
Literature by Doing, *Tchudi & Yesner*
Lively Writing, *Schrank*
Look, Think & Write, *Leavitt & Sohn*
NTC Shakespeare Series
NTC Vocabulary Builders
Poetry by Doing, *Osborn*
World Literature, *Rosenberg*
Write to the Point! *Morgan*
The Writer's Handbook, *Karls & Szymanski*
Writing by Doing, *Sohn & Enger*
Writing in Action, *Meredith*

Media Communication
Getting Started in Mass Media, *Beckert*
Photography in Focus, *Jacobs & Kokrda*
Television Production Today!, *Bielak*
Understanding Mass Media, *Jawitz*
Understanding the Film, *Bone & Johnson*

Mythology
The Ancient World, *Sawyer & Townsend*
Mythology and You, *Rosenberg & Baker*
Welcome to Ancient Greece, *Millard*
Welcome to Ancient Rome, *Millard*
World Mythology, *Rosenberg*

Speech
Activities for Effective Communication, *LiSacchi*
The Basics of Speech, *Galvin, Cooper, & Gordon*
Contemporary Speech, *HopKins & Whitaker*
Creative Speaking, *Frank*
Dynamics of Speech, *Myers & Herndon*
Getting Started in Oral Interpretation, *Naegelin &*
Krikac
Getting Started in Public Speaking, *Carlin & Payne*
Listening by Doing, *Galvin*
Literature Alive, *Gamble & Gamble*
Person to Person, *Galvin & Book*
Public Speaking Today, *Carlin & Payne*
Speaking by Doing, *Buys, Sill, & Beck*

Theatre
Acting & Directing, *Grandstaff*
The Book of Cuttings for Acting & Directing,
Cassady
The Book of Monologues for Aspiring Actors,
Cassady
The Book of Scenes for Acting Practice, *Cassady*
The Book of Scenes for Aspiring Actors, *Cassady*
The Dynamics of Acting, *Snyder & Drumsta*
Getting Started in Theatre, *Pinnell*
An Introduction to Modern One-Act Plays, *Cassady*
An Introduction to Theatre and Drama, *Cassady &*
Cassady
Play Production Today, *Beck et al.*
Stagecraft, *Beck*

For a current catalog and information about our complete line of language
arts books, write:
National Textbook Company
a division of *NTC Publishing Group*
4255 West Touhy Avenue
Lincolnwood (Chicago), Illinois 60646–1975 U.S.A.